The Characteristics and Needs of Adults in Postsecondary Education

The Characteristics and Needs of Adults in Postsecondary Education

Lewis C. Solmon
University of California at
Los Angeles and
Higher Education Research
Institute, Inc.

Joanne J. Gordon
Higher Education Research
Institute, Inc.

LexingtonBooks
D.C. Heath and Company
Lexington, Massachusetts
Toronto

The research report herein was performed pursuant to a grant from the National Institute of Education, U.S. Department of Health, Education, and Welfare (Contract #400-78-0046). Contractors undertaking such projects under Government sponsorship are encouraged to express freely their professional judgment in the conduct of the project. Points of view or opinions stated do not, therefore, necessarily represent official National Institute of Education position or policy.

Library of Congress Cataloging in Publication Data

Solmon, Lewis C
   The characteristics and needs of adults in postsecondary education.

   Includes bibliographical references.
   1. Continuing education—United States. 2. Adult education—United States. I. Gordon, Joanne J., joint author. II. Title.
LC5251.S64   378'.1554   80-8782
ISBN 0-669-04361-3

Copyright © 1981 by D.C. Heath and Company

Published simultaneously in Canada

Printed in the United States of America

International Standard Book Number: 0-669-04361-3

Library of Congress Catalog Card Number: 80-8782

To
Eva and Eddie Solmon
and
Seemah and Frank Gordon

Contents

	List of Tables	ix
	Acknowledgments	xv
Chapter 1	Introduction	1
Chapter 2	Demographics	9
	Enrollment Status	9
	Age	13
	Sex Differences	13
	Racial Background	16
	Marital Status	20
	Number of Children	24
	Father's and Mother's Educational Attainment	24
Chapter 3	College Choice	27
	Types of Institutions Attended as Freshmen	27
	Why College Students Selected the College They Attended	31
Chapter 4	Financing of College Education	39
Chapter 5	Preparation for College	51
	Curriculum Preparation in High School	52
	Remedial Help	53
	High-School Grade-Point Average	54
Chapter 6	College Plans	59
	Living Arrangements	59
	Degree Aspirations	62
	Probable Major	63
	Institutional Quality	69
	Probable Career Occupation	70
Chapter 7	Life Goals	73
	Important Objectives for Adult Students	73
	Important Objectives for Traditional-Age Students	75

Least Important Objectives for Adult Students   75
Least Important Objectives for Traditional-Age
    Students   75
Artistic Objectives   76
Status Objectives   76
Social Objectives   76
Family Objectives   77
Business Objectives   77
Personal Objectives   77
Multivariate Analysis   78
Summary   82

Chapter 8   Implications: Accommodating New Clients   85

Appendix A   Supplementary Tables   99

Appendix B   1977 Follow-Up of the 1970 Freshman Cohort   113

               References   141

               Index   145

               About the Authors   157

List of Tables

1-1   Comparison of Norms Participants and Number of Freshman in the CIRP Data Base Who Are Age 21, by Survey Year   6

2-1   Enrollment Status of Adult Respondents, by Year and Sex   10

2-2   Enrollment Status of Adult Respondents, by Year and Type of Institution   11

2-3   Enrollment Status of Adult Respondents, for all Institutions, by Year   12

2-4   Ages of Adult Respondents, by Year   14

2-5   Distribution of Adult Men and Women, for All Institutions, by Year   15

2-6   Percentage of Adults Over Age 25, by Year and Sex   16

2-7   Institutional Type and Enrollment Status of Adult Respondents, by Year and Sex   17

2-8   Race for all Institutions, by Year and Student Type (Traditional and Adult)   18

2-9   Race of Adult Respondents, for Institutional Type, by Sex and Year   20

2-10   Race for All Institutions, by Year, Sex, and Student Type (Traditional and Adult)   21

2-11   Enrollment Status of Adult Respondents, by Year and Race   22

2-12   Characteristics of Adult Respondents, by Marital Status   23

3-1   Adult and Traditional Students in Postsecondary Education, by Year and Type of Institution   28

3-2   Choice of College for All Institutions, by Year and Student Type (Traditional and Adult)   30

3-3   Reasons Noted as "Very Important" in Selecting this College, for All Institutions, by Year and Student Type (Traditional and Adult)   32

3-4   Reasons Noted as "Very Important" in Selecting Type of College, for 1978 (Traditional and Adult)   33

3-5   Reasons Noted as "Very Important" in Selecting this Particular College, for Adult Respondents, by Enrollment Status and Year   36

4-1   Financial Concerns of Respondents, for All Institutions, by Year and Student Type (Traditional and Adult)   40

4-2   Source of Financing First Year of College, for All Institutions, by Year and Student Type (Traditional and Adult)   42

4-3   Source of Financing College Education for Adult Respondents, for All Institutions, by Year   44

4-4   Correlates with Concern about Ability to Finance College Education   45

5-1   Type of High-School Program, for All Institutions, by Year and Student Type (Traditional and Adult)   52

5-2   "Poor Curriculum Preparation at My High School," for Adult Respondents, for All Institutions, by Year   52

5-3   "Perceived Need of Tutoring," for All Institutions, by Year and Student Type (Traditional and Adult)   54

5-4   High-School Grade-Point Average, for All Institutions, by Year and Student Type (Traditional and Adult)   55

5-5   Year Adult and Traditional-Age Respondents Graduated from High School, for All Institutions, by Year   56

5-6   Courses Taken by Adult Respondents at Any Other Institution, by Enrollment Status and Year   57

5-7   Courses Taken for Credit by Adult Respondents at this Institution, by Enrollment Status and Year   58

6-1   Distance from Home to College of Adult Respondents, by Year and Sex   60

6-2   Miles from Home and Where Plan to Live Next Fall, for All Institutions, by Year and Student Type (Traditional and Adult)   61

6-3	Living Arrangements of Adult Respondents, by Enrollment Status and Year	63
6-4	Highest Degree Planned Anywhere, for All Institutions, by Year and Student Type (Traditional and Adult)	64
6-5	Highest Degree Planned for Adult Respondents, by Type of Institution and Year	65
6-6	Highest Degree Planned for Adult Respondents, by Enrollment Status and Year	66
6-7	Marital Status of Adult Respondents, by Highest Degree Planned and Year	67
6-8	Probable Major, for All Institutions, by Year and Student Type (Traditional and Adult)	68
6-9	Probable Major for 1978 Adult Respondents, by Type of Institution	69
6-10	Probable Major of Adult Respondents, by Enrollment Status and Year	70
6-11	Probable Career Occupation, for All Institutions, by Year and Student Type (Traditional and Adult)	71
6-12	Probable Career Occupation of Adult Respondents, by Enrollment Status and Year	72
7-1	Objectives Considered "Essential" or "Very Important," for All Institutions, by Year and Student Type (Traditional and Adult)	74
7-2	Correlates with Life Goals	79
7-3	Objectives Considered by Adult Respondents "Essential" or "Very Important," by Enrollment Status and Year	81
A-1	Reasons Noted by Adult Male Respondents as "Very Important" in Selecting this College, by Marital Status, Year, and Sex	100
A-2	Reasons Noted by Adult Female Respondents as "Very Important" in Selecting this College, by Marital Status, Year, and Sex	101
A-3	Financial Concern of Adult Respondents, by Marital Status and Year	102

A-4   Financial Concern of Adult Respondents, by Year and
       Enrollment Status   103

A-5   Source of First Year's Educational Expenses for
       White Adult Respondents, by Type of Institution and
       Year   104

A-6   Source of First Year's Educational Expenses for Black
       Adult Respondents, by Type of Institution and Year   105

A-7   Source of First Year's Educational Expenses for
       "Other" Adult Respondents, by Type of Institution
       and Year   106

A-8   Source of First Year's Educational Expenses of Adult
       Respondents, by Year and Enrollment Status   107

A-9   Source of First Year's Educational Expenses for Adult
       Respondents, by Marital Status and Year   108

A-10   Source of First Year's Educational Expenses for Male
       Adult Respondents, by Marital Status and Year   109

A-11   Source of First Year's Educational Expenses for
       Female Adult Respondents, by Marital Status and
       Year   110

A-12   Source of First Year's Educational Expenses for Adult
       Respondents, by Father's Educational Attainment and
       Year   111

A-13   Probable Major of Adult Respondents, by Marital
       Status and Year   112

B-1   Very Important Factors in Decision to Attend
       College, by Age   114

B-2   Tuition of College for 1970 Freshmen, by Age   115

B-3   Highest Degree Planned When Entered College, by
       Highest Degree Held in 1977 and Age   117

B-4   Very Important Factors in Selecting Undergraduate
       Major as Reported in 1977, by Age   118

B-5   Types of College Counseling Received, by Age   120

B-6   Satisfaction with Types of College Counseling
       Received, by Age   120

B-7   Whether or Not 1970 College Was the Same as the
       Last College Attended, by Age   121

B-8   Satisfaction with Colleges Attended, by Age   121

B-9   Usefulness of a College Education, by Age   122

B-10   Attitudes toward the Statement, "The Chief Benefit
           of a College Education Is that It Increases One's
           Earning Power," by Age   123

B-11   Change in Attitude from 1970 to 1977 toward the
           Statement, "The Chief Benefit of a College Education
           Is that It Increases One's Earning Power," by Age   124

B-12   Changes Would Make if Considering College Today
           (with Present Experience and Knowledge), by Age   125

B-13   Employment while in College, by Age   126

B-14   When Made Career Choice, by Age   126

B-15   Job Search Methods that Worked in Getting Current
           or Most Recent Job, for Full-Time Employees, by
           Age   127

B-16   Current Occupation of Full-Time Employees, by Age   128

B-17   Relation of Current or Most Recent Job to
           Undergraduate Major, for Full-Time Employees, by
           Age   129

B-18   Reasons Working in a Job Only Somewhat or Not
           Related to Undergraduate Major, for Full-Time
           Employees, by Age   130

B-19   Extent of Contribution of Various Experiences to
           Current or Most Recent Job, for Full-Time
           Employees, by Age   131

B-20   Job Characteristics of Full-Time Employees, by Age   132

B-21   Current Annual Income of Full-Time Employees
           before Taxes, by Age   133

B-22   Attitudes of Full-Time Employees toward Work, by
           Age   134

B-23   Perceptions of Underemployment, for Full-Time
           Employees, by Age   135

B-24   Satisfaction of Full-Time Employees with Current or
           Most Recent Job, by Age   135

B-25   Whether or Not Working in a Preferred Occupation,
             for Full-Time Employees, by Age   136

B-26   Degree of Satisfaction of Full-Time Employees with
             Various Aspects of Current or Most Recent Job, by
             Age   137

B-27   Career Plans of Full-Time Employees, by Age   138

B-28   Change in Career Plans of Full-Time Employees, by
             Age   139

B-29   Satisfaction with Various Aspects of Life, by Age   139

Acknowledgments

The idea for this book originated at a meeting organized by Nevzer Stacey that was held by the National Institute of Education (NIE). NIE provided funds for our research and Ms. Stacey was a constant source of strength and substance for us throughout the project. As the research evolved toward completion, many who heard or read our reports provided useful insights. In particular, Ivan Charner of the National Manpower Institute (formerly of NIE) was helpful at several points; our colleague at the Higher Education Research Institute, Ann Bisconti, provided many useful suggestions; and Kathleen Rockhill of the University of California at Los Angeles made extensive comments and suggestions on a late draft of the manuscript.

When this project started, Nancy L. Ochsner served as a senior associate. Her contributions to the formative stages of the book were valuable and helped us begin on the right foot. As usual, various members of the Higher Education Research Institute provided the support services—typing, programming, and more—that have enabled this book to be written.

A major vote of thanks is due to our friend Alexander W. Astin, who developed the thirteen years of freshman surveys upon which our study is based. His role in providing higher education researchers with the data base to study the students of our institutions cannot be overestimated.

Finally, one of us would like to pay special tribute to Vicki R. Solmon, J.D., who has been successful both as a traditional college student and as an adult who returned to law school. Her travails as an adult woman student made at least one of us sensitive to the issues discussed in this report and provided concrete examples of the barriers faced by many thousands of her counterparts.

Some of those who have provided input may not be completely satisfied with the product. Unfortunately, data were not available to enable us to address all the issues that should have been raised in a study of adults in college. This book is only a beginning, and all errors of omission as well as those of commission are the responsibility of the authors.

1   Introduction

A major issue for colleges and universities to confront today is whether the accelerated enrollment rate of entering or reentering adult students (those over the age of 21) can or will compensate for the projected declining enrollment of traditional-age college students (the 18-to-21-year-olds). The issue involves not only whether there are enough adults to fill the empty places, but also whether the adults' educational needs can be met by institutions originally established to educate younger students. Many scholars interested in adult access to postsecondary education have commented on this issue.

> Whether sufficient millions of adults will be forthcoming to offset the expected enrollment decline among 18-to-21-year-olds is problematic. Thus far, the large majority of adults is enrolling in non-degree programs taught by faculty below the doctoral level in community colleges. This new audience may not prove an adequate substitute for full-time undergraduates of traditional age and with traditional degree interests. (Cartter and Solmon 1976, p. 38)

If adults are turning to nondegree programs in community colleges, traditional colleges and universities may not be meeting their needs adequately. Some changes may be required.

Some scholars believe that the traditional educational system is flexible enough in its present state to accommodate adult students (Church 1978; Eldred and Marienau 1979). Harrington (1977) says, "The historical record shows that fitting adults into the academic pattern does not require a complete—and therefore disturbing or impossible—transformation of post-secondary education and its values" (p. 10). Until now, very little information has been available to clarify this issue.

Although there is a considerable amount of literature on adults in higher education, most of it is outdated. The evening college movement was studied during the 1950s. Much recent literature refers to developmental aspects of adult learning (Knox 1977) or to the problems of accommodating the elderly on campus (Weinstock 1978). Noticeably absent from the existing literature are adequate descriptions of major trends in adult postsecondary education. Even when this information is available, it is national in scope and offers little guidance to administrators of traditional programs who are concerned with adult needs at the local level (Kuh and Ardaiolo, 1979; Arbeiter 1977). Also, the tendency to consider as a whole

1

the different groups of adult learners (that is, full-time and part-time, and degree-seeking and nondegree-seeking students) obscures the actual number of potential learners in various groups (Kuh and Ardaiolo 1979).

The various definitions of adult students in the existing literature make it difficult to compare information. Much of the literature takes an age cut-off approach: An adult or nontraditional student in higher education is distinguished from his traditional counterpart merely by his age, regardless of educational status. The traditional-college-age student usually is defined to include only 18-to-22-year-olds. Therefore, nontraditional students are those over age 22 (Harrington 1977; Schlaver 1977; Shulman 1976; Rossmann 1979).

Another distinction often made is based on type of educational participation rather than, or in addition to, age. Basic differentiations are made between full-time and part-time students, between degree and nondegree students, or according to where the education is obtained. The Indiana Commission for Higher Education (1979) is one of the few organizations to classify students 17 or older as adults for educational purposes (Anderson and Darkenwald 1979). That is, students of what is normally considered traditional college age are viewed as adults, depending upon the nature of their participation.

The National Center for Education Statistics (NCES) distinguishes between "adult education" and "adults in education." Adult education refers to "organized learning to meet the unique needs of persons beyond compulsory school age who have terminated or interrupted their formal schooling" (NCES 1978a). "Courses taken by full-time students in high school or college as part of their regular curriculum were not to be reported as adult education," but if a full-time high school or college student took swimming instruction at a local community center, for example, he was counted as a participant in adult education. Using this definition, NCES estimated that the number of adult education students "who were not full-time students in high school or college increased from 13,041,000 in 1969 to 17,059,000 in 1975 (a 30.8 percent increase during the six-year period, or an average annual increase of 4.6 percent)." During this same time, they estimated, "the number of adults attending high school or college on a *full-time* basis increased 4.0 percent, or at an annual rate of 0.7 percent," resulting in an additional 1,013,000 adult students in high school or college. This brings the total number of participants to 18,072,000, or 12.3 percent of the total adult population (NCES 1978a).

If this number of part-time adult education students (17,059,000) represents a "market" for two- and four-year colleges, it would indicate an exceedingly optimistic future for traditional postsecondary institutions. In 1975 the total full-time-equivalent (FTE) enrollment in all institutions of higher education was only 8,481,000 (NCES 1978b). That is, the figure cited by NCES (17,059,000) representing the potential additional market would be twice the FTE enrollment for 1975 of 8,481,000. Even this figure, however, would not represent the real adult market for traditional colleges. It includes many who should not be considered in the potential college market and it excludes many who should be considered. Some of the courses taken by adult education students are not offered by traditional colleges and universities. Other courses may be available through extension programs at traditional colleges but they may not be taught by the regular faculty. Furthermore, although NCES includes students under 21 in their definition of adult education students, most colleges and universities consider this age group as their traditional clientele.

NCES excludes from its definition students over 21 enrolled full- or part-time in college but not taking extension courses. Surely this group represents a "market" for traditional colleges.

A report prepared by K. Patricia Cross on adult learners' characteristics, needs, and interests uses the NCES definition of adult learners. She comments that "this definition has the advantage of conforming rather nicely to the common perception of what is meant by adult learners and adult learning activities but . . . definitions limited to 'organized' learning activities result in quite conservative statistics" (Cross and Valley 1976, p. 76).

This book is primarily concerned with adult participants in traditional postsecondary educational institutions, most of whom would be pursuing traditional degrees. However the different forms that the education of adults can take and alternatives to formal institutions of postsecondary education will also be discussed.

We examined a landmark study on participation, conducted by J.W.C. Johnstone and R.J. Rivera in 1965, in estimating the number of adults engaged in educational activities, however that investigation was concerned with "all activities consciously and systematically organized for purposes of acquiring new knowledge, information, and skills" (p. 1) and covered a much wider range of activities than is usually associated with the term adult education. The adult population was defined to include persons who were either 21 or over, married, or the head of a household.

From the viewpoint of the colleges and universities, the potential adult clientele refers to those over 21 who might enroll either full or part time in regular college courses taught by the regular faculty. The adult students may or may not plan to take courses for credit or apply them toward a degree. These students, then, would be called "adults in postsecondary education" rather than "participants in adult education"—two very different groups.

Estimates of the general population of students in college in 1978 were available from the Bureau of the Census (1979) in their *Current Population*

Reports. Age breakdowns in these reports are similar to the age breakdowns in our data. In October 1978 there were 16,245,000 18-to-21-year-olds in the general population, with 5,197,000, or 32 percent, of them in college. Of the 44,682,000 22-to-34-year-olds in the general population, 4,367,000, or 10 percent, were in college. Two million seven hundred and thirty-nine thousand 22-to-34-year-olds were undergraduates. Of these adults who were undergraduates, 1,380,000 of them were enrolled full time and 1,359,000 were enrolled part time. We do not know which year of college these students were enrolled in or whether they were taking regular college courses taught by regular faculty. However these figures do show that in October of 1978 there were 40 million adults aged 22 to 34 who were not enrolled in college. Many of these adults as well as adults over 34 are future students at traditional colleges and universities.

To examine these estimates in more detail and to look at trends over time, the figures available in both 1972 and 1978 are broken down into two age categories—25-to-34, and 35-and-over. The population is so grouped because we define the adults in our sample as those over 21, and the *Current Population Reports* include all years of college, not just the freshman year. So the traditional-age student population (in any of the four college years) includes students who may be as old as 24. Hence the total adult student population refers to those who are 25 and over. Also, trends over time can be reviewed for the adult students without irregularities attributable to the effects of the GI Bill: Many college students in their early twenties are not returning adults but merely traditional students who have delayed entry by a year or two because of military service. As we shall see, this group has declined significantly as the number of Vietnam war veterans returning to college has diminished.

Between 1972 and 1978 there was an increase of almost 1.5 million in the adult student population (25 or over). The increase in the traditional-age cohort between these two years was only seven hundred thousand. Although this comparison appears to have important policy implications, it must be remembered that even though the potential market for traditional postsecondary institutions is huge, there are already over a million and a half adults in college. So if, for example, one million full-time-equivalent adults are needed to offset the declining number of traditional-age students, and if it takes five adult part-time students to make up for one full-time traditional-age student, with respect to demands on regular daytime faculty (Cartter and Solmon 1976), five million adults will have to be recruited. And these will not be the adults most inclined toward college attendance, because the million and a half adults most likely to attend are already attending. So to compensate for declining enrollments of new high-school graduates, several million *more* adults must be attracted.

In both 1972 and 1978 there were twice as many adults in the 25-to-34 age group as in the 35-and-over group. In 1972, 19 percent of college students were 25-to-34-year-olds and 9 percent were 35 and over; in 1978, 23 percent were 25-to-34-year-olds and 12 percent were 35 and over. By 1978, 35 percent of all college attenders were at least 25 years old. However the growth rate is probably higher for the older group.

In 1972 29 percent of the men in college were 25 or over, whereas only 26 percent of the women were 25 or over. However, by 1978 the proportion of adult women was greater than the proportion of adult men (33 percent of the men were 25 or over compared with 36 percent of the women). The proportion of adult women grew much more quickly than the proportion of adult men.

Most traditional-age undergraduate students (24 and under) enrolled in college full time (88 percent in 1972 and 84 percent in 1978) whereas most adult students (25-to-34) enrolled part time (59 percent in 1972 and 63 percent in 1978). Interesting differences in the enrollment status of adult and traditional-age students are discernible when examined by institutional type. Over twice as many adults aged 25 to 34 in four-year colleges attended full time as compared with those in two-year colleges. Similarly, many more traditional-age students in two-year colleges (as compared with those in four-year colleges) attended part time.

Although these figures are instructive, some caution must be taken when comparing them with data reported below. We do not know how many of the adults represented in the *Current Population Reports* have progressed beyond the freshman year. However, in many cases, the part-time status of adults would lead them to spend several years in what might traditionally be viewed as the freshman year of college. So our sample of freshman adults might be more representative of all adults in college than our sample of younger freshman is representative of all traditional-age college attenders. The summary statistics from the *Current Population Reports*, however, do provide some basis on which to evaluate the representativeness of our sample.

Given the actual and potential numbers of adults in undergraduate education, we need to know more about them as students and how they compare with their traditional counterparts. Our study of first-year college students will provide us with more detail on similarities and differences between adult and traditional-age college attenders.

If colleges and universities want to evaluate adults as a potential expanding market, they must determine which, if any, administrative and curricular changes would have to be made to better meet the educational needs of these older students and to attract greater numbers of over-21-year-olds. In what kinds of programs and institutions do adults enroll? What are their educational goals and expectations, their priorities in life, their financial and educational needs? Are the adults attending college today different from those who attended five or ten years ago?

If adult and traditional-age students have similar characteristics, attend comparable institutions, and have comparable needs, goals, and expectations, few changes in postsecondary education will be required to accommodate this new clientele. On the other hand, if these two groups are substantially different, and if increased adult student enrollments are sought to offset the projected declining enrollments of traditional-age students, the higher-education system will have to change.

To assess the similarities and differences between adult and traditional-age students, the Higher Education Research Institute (HERI) analyzed the survey responses of thirteen cohorts of first-year college freshmen. Since 1966, the Cooperative Institutional Research Program (CIRP) has annually surveyed students entering approximately six hundred colleges across the United States. Each year the responses have been weighted and results have been compiled into a national norms series (1966-78). The CIRP norms are based only on responses for first-time, full-time freshmen from institutions with high response rates.

The CIRP samples include a significant number (51,085) of first-time, full-time adults (see table 1-1). In this book we have used responses of all CIRP adult (over age 21) freshmen, a larger number than reported in the

Table 1-1
Comparison of Norms Participants and Number of Freshmen in the CIRP Data Base Who Are Age 21, by Survey Year

Survey Year	Number of CIRP Norms Participants	Estimated Number of Freshmen Over Age 21[a]	Actual Number of Freshmen Over Age 21
1966	206,865	3,413[b]	6,007
1967	185,848	3,527	8,629
1968	243,156	5,947	8,525
1969	169,190	4,974	9,568
1970	180,684	6,478	8,006
1971	171,509	4,448	13,571
1972	188,900	3,973	15,854
1973	189,733	2,901	17,125
1974	189,724	2,905	19,709
1975	186,406	2,969	20,270
1976	215,890	3,005	17,687
1977	198,641	2,981	15,558
1978	187,603	3,564	13,903
Total	2,514,149	51,085	172,400

[a]Norms data included only first-time, full-time freshmen selected from institutions which meet certain criteria.

[b]Estimated on the basis of the percentage of freshmen who were over the age of 21 in 1966.

published norms because it includes part-timers, returning students, and those from institutions with response rates too low to be reported in the norms. In particular, the CIRP institutions that have the lowest overall response rates are two-year colleges. Because two-year colleges attract many adult students, and specifically, many adults who are poor, of minority racial or ethnic background, and less prepared than their traditional counterparts, the CIRP data probably underrepresent adult freshmen from that sector and those special groups from within that sector. The thirteen years of CIRP surveys produced a sample of 172,400 adult freshmen, the largest group of adults in colleges for which data have ever been collected.

Some observers argue that adult education typically reaches the most highly educated, whites, and the more affluent. It is difficult, therefore, to determine whether the results presented in this book reflect biases in our sampling procedure, or whether minorities are over- or underrepresented. Although blacks might be overrepresented vis-à-vis the total population in adult education (broadly defined), they are probably underrepresented vis-à-vis the actual population of adults in two- or four-year colleges. Nevertheless, when results are reported separately by institutional type, we expect our findings for these subgroups to be representative.

To reiterate: Whether our adult sample is representative of the total population of adult freshmen is uncertain because appropriate national statistics are not available on a disaggregated basis. When we compare the adults to the traditional CIRP norms samples, the differences we find are probably understated because the norms exclude part-time freshmen (so the part-time responses in our adult samples were obtained spuriously) and because some of the first-time, full-time adults were included in both the norms and the adult comparisons.

To expand the scope of information available from the existing literature and the previously described data, the results of an analysis of a subgroup of adult and traditional-age graduates from the 1977 CIRP follow-up survey of the 1970 freshman cohort are presented in Appendix B. The results and their implications for institutional policies affecting adult learners are discussed. The focus is on what the research tells us about the special needs and demands of adult learners. We hope to increase the awareness of those involved in student affairs and related services. However, results from this analysis cannot be generalized to all adults in postsecondary education because the sample of adults from the follow-up study is quite small and because the respondents were randomly selected and not necessarily representative of all those who responded to the 1970 survey.

2

Demographics

Adults constitute a large and growing segment of the population of our colleges and universities, yet until now very little has been known about their educational needs and goals. If higher-education institutions are to regard adult students as substitutes for the decreasing numbers of traditional-age students, they need to know how the adult and traditional students are different. Do adults have the same high-school preparation as their traditional-age counterparts? Are they more likely to enroll part time rather than full time? To need more or different kinds of financial assistance? To need more remedial help? To come from minority backgrounds or to be women rather than men? Are adults more likely to choose a college by its location rather than by its reputation? Are they likely to select the same majors and want the same kinds of courses as traditional freshmen?

Enrollment Status

Because the CIRP reports data only on first-time, full-time freshmen, comparisons of the adults' enrollment tendencies with those of the traditional-age students must be examined with caution. The CIRP data collection procedures as well as its reporting format tend to exclude part-time students and those who attend classes in the evening because the CIRP questionnaires are usually distributed during freshman orientation or registration for the traditional day students. Also, the classification of full- and part-time enrollment depends on institutional policies, so technically these classifications may not be consistent from institution to institution. However, the Bureau of the Census (1979) estimates that in 1978, 75 percent of all two-year college attenders and 53 percent of all four-year college attenders between the ages of 25 and 34 were enrolled part time. We have full-time/part-time information on our freshman adult sample only for the years 1972-1978. In those years the number of adults enrolled part time ranged from 20 to 26 percent for all CIRP institutions combined.[a] This con-

---

[a]We do not mean to imply that the part-time/full-time rates reported for the CIRP adult sample are representative of all adults in postsecondary education. We have shown that the part-time rate for all adults is much higher. However, it is likely that data reported are representative for part-timers and full-timers separately, and changes reported over time might be indicative of national trends. In many cases throughout this report, data are presented separately by enrollment status. When data are not presented separately by enrollment status, there may be biases because of the overrepresentation of full-time adults.

firms a bias in the CIRP adult data. Generally, adults apply for admission as part-time students so that they can continue working while going to school (Harrington 1977). Adult students do not rely on financial aid as much as traditional-age students but tend to rely instead on their own incomes to finance their educations.

Despite the bias toward full-timers in the CIRP data, sex differences, and trends over time are probably in the right direction. Women (especially those who are married and living with their spouses) were more likely to enroll part time than men, but between 1974 and 1978 (the two years we chose to show comparisons over time) the proportion of adult females who enrolled full time increased more (from 66 to 73 percent) than the proportion of adult males (see table 2-1). Before 1974 women were probably more restricted in their freedom to attend college full time because of the prevalent attitude in society that women should be responsible for child care and the belief that older women's aspirations should not include pursuing higher education. Recently, however, attitudes toward women's roles have been changing.

Adult freshmen in two-year colleges were more likely than those in four-year colleges and universities to attend part-time. Part-time enrollment in two-year colleges ranges from approximately 21 to 36 percent. Public colleges and universities enroll a larger number of part-time adult freshmen than private colleges and universities.

Between 1974 and 1978 the proportion of full-time adults in two-year colleges increased substantially, from 64 percent to 72 percent (see table 2-2). In most other kinds of institutions, the proportion remained the same or decreased slightly. Perhaps four-year institutions are becoming more receptive to part-time students because of declining enrollment rates, but until we know whether our adult samples are representative of the total adult freshman population, we cannot be certain about these part-time/full-time trends.

Between 1967 and 1969, two-thirds of our adult students were in college for the first time (see table 2-3). In 1971 the number decreased to about 50 percent, and by 1978 to 28 percent. All of the relevant literature on adults in

Table 2-1
Enrollment Status of Adult Respondents, by Year and Sex
(in percentages)

	1974		1978	
	Part-time	*Full-time*	*Part-time*	*Full-time*
Males	20	80	16	84
Females	34	66	27	73

Table 2-2

Enrollment Status of Adult Respondents, by Year and Type of Institution
(in percentages)

	1974		1978	
	Part-time	Full-time	Part-time	Full-time
All two-year colleges	36	64	28	72
All four-year colleges	17	83	21	79
All universities	14	86	13	87
Predominantly black colleges	19	81	25	75
Two-year colleges (public)	37	63	29	71
Two-year colleges (private)	17	83	11	89
Four-year colleges (public)	23	77	31	69
Four-year colleges (private)	12	88	8	92
Four-year colleges (Protestant)	6	94	9	91
Four-year colleges (Catholic)	11	89	20	80
Public universities	16	85	14	86
Private universities	9	91	10	90
Predominantly black colleges (public)	21	79	19	81
Predominantly black colleges (private)	5	95	35	65

postsecondary education confirms that those with more education tend to seek more education (Schlaver 1977; Knox 1977; Cross and Valley 1976). There is more participation in postsecondary education by college graduates or those who have had some previous college background than by those with less schooling. Johnstone and Rivera (1965) point out that "somewhere in the process of getting an education, it seems people learn either that education itself is a continuing life experience, or that the way to acquire new skills and knowledge in life is to engage in formal or informal programs of study" (p. 104).

Also, well-educated adults are often in professional white-collar jobs that encourage continued learning. Promotions and salary increases in such occupations are often conditional upon academic course work and employers frequently pay tuition costs (Bishop and Van Dyk 1977; Schlaver 1977). Adults with less education tend to be in blue-collar jobs that do not require more formal learning (London, Wenkert, and Hagstrom 1963). Perhaps the employers of blue-collar workers discourage the pursuit of further education because increased knowledge could lead to higher aspirations and therefore increase job dissatisfaction.

Much of the human capital literature also claims that those with the most education are the most likely to further augment their human capital through the acquistion of on-the-job training (Mincer 1970). One reason for this is that those with more education are more efficient in converting schooling into productive human capital. To rectify this imbalance, Wirtz

Table 2-3
Enrollment Status of Adult Respondents, for All Institutions, by Year
(in percentages)

	1966	1967	1968	1969	1970	1971	1972	1973	1974	1975	1976	1977	1978
First-time freshmen	—	65	69	68	100	54	—	—	—	—	—	—	—
Full-time							32	25	23	23	23	23	22
Part-time							9	7	8	7	6	6	6
Attended college before—													
Now full-time							48	52	51	53	58	56	56
Now part-time							11	16	18	17	14	15	16
Transfer from junior college		16	16	17		17							
Transfer from four-year college		19	15	15		16							
Courses for credit here							23	24	23	26	22	18	21
No credit elsewhere							48	33	21	19	17	17	18
Credit at junior college							22	23	25	25	27	27	29
Credit at four-year college							23	24	23	22	25	25	26
Credit at other postsecondary institution							14	11	12	13	13	14	14
No credit elsewhere								24	22	24	24	22	21
Junior college, no credit								3	4	5	6	5	5
Four-year college, no credit								3	3	5	5	5	4
Other postsecondary institution, no credit								13	15	16	16	15	15

(1964) suggests that substantial efforts be directed toward increasing training opportunities for workers with the lowest educational levels. Nevertheless, if the trend is real—if increasing proportions of adults are returning to college—institutions may need to reevaluate their course-credit transfer policies. By 1978 more than 80 percent of adult freshmen had taken courses for credit at other institutions.

Age

Discussion of the age of adults in postsecondary education is confused by the different breakdowns used by various scholars in their attempts to differentiate between traditional and nontraditional students. The largest adult group that has pursued postsecondary education comprises people in their twenties and thirties (Boaz 1978; Wiggins 1977; and Hamilton 1978), with few older than their mid-fifties. Recent trends indicate that more people over fifty are attending college, but that they are generally not in degree-credit programs. Knox (1977) suggests that "beyond age sixty, adults continue to read materials that are readily available, but there is a decline in use of print media that must be obtained outside the home, such as books from libraries and book stores" (p. 174).

Many of those classified as adult students in this book are close in age to those classified as traditional students. This may blur important distinctions, but we cannot determine fine age breakdowns for our adult samples because the CIRP questionnaires had only very broad categories beyond age 21. All those over the age of 21 were in one category. None of the pre-1970 samples had the categories 22-to-25-years-old and 26-and-over.

From 1970 to 1973, most adult freshmen were between 22 and 25 years old (see table 2-4). The percentage of adult freshmen over 25 increased from 38 percent in 1970 to 49 percent in 1978. This increase could be explained by the more accepting attitude in society toward adults in college in recent years. Or, perhaps the concentration of adults in the 22-to-25-year-old range in the early 1970s reflects the tendency for armed forces veterans to enter college after leaving active service.

Sex Differences

Over the years there has been a dramatic increase in the representation of women in the adult sample (see table 2-5). Although we are unable to determine whether the increase in the percentage of women (from 29 to 57 percent) between 1966 and 1978 is a result of CIRP sampling methods or a reflection of a real trend, we suspect it is at least in part the latter. If this

Table 2-4
Ages of Adult Respondents, by Year
(in percentages)

Year	Age 22-25	Age 26 and Over
1970	62	38
1971	63	37
1972	58	42
1973	53	48
1974	48	51
1975	47	53
1976	53	47
1977	52	48
1978	51	49

Data not available prior to 1970.

trend is representative, it could confirm the general belief that more and more women are participating in higher education because of the greater encouragement offered to them in recent years to pursue their educational and career goals (Westervelt 1975).

Table 2-6 indicates that adult women in postsecondary education tend to be older than adult men. In most years, approximately 60 percent of the adult women in the CIRP adult sample were over 26, compared with approximately 40 percent of the adult men. This is probably due in part to the fact that some men were serving in the military in the early years of the sample. It might also be that men begin work at an early age and upon realizing the value of a college education decide to go to school, whereas women are forced or deliberately elect to stay out of school until they are older.

Table 2-7 presents the proportions of adults of each sex who were part-time and full-time students from 1972 to 1978 by institutional type. Overall, men were much more likely to be attending full time (over 80 percent were full-time, compared with about 70 percent of women). In almost all years, adult men and women in the predominantly black colleges were the most likely to be full-timers. Also, in black colleges differences in enrollment status between men and women were the smallest.

Adults in two-year colleges were most likely to be attending part-time, and many more women than men attended part time. Again, we are tempted to explain sex differences in enrollment status by the multiple commitments of women. Historically women have taken primary responsibility for childrearing and women have often worked part time so their husbands could attend college full time. The need for effective, low-cost, child-care facilities, increased financial aid availability, and changes in society's expec-

Table 2-5
Distribution of Adult Men and Women, for All Institutions, by Year

	1966	1967	1968	1969	1970	1971	1972	1973	1974	1975	1976	1977	1978
Men	4,241	5,936	5,884	6,635	5,476	8,771	9,905	10,129	10,447	10,909	9,011	7,324	6,018
Women	1,712	2,693	2,641	2,951	2,530	4,300	5,949	6,996	9,262	9,361	8,676	8,234	7,885
Percentage of Women	29	31	31	31	32	33	38	41	47	46	49	53	57

Table 2-6
Percentage of Adults Over Age 25, by Year and Sex

	Males	Females
1970	27	62
1971	27	57
1972	33	58
1973	39	60
1974	43	62
1975	46	60
1976	39	56
1977	38	56
1978	37	57

Data unavailable for the years prior to 1970.

tations of women are obvious if adult women are to be given equal opportunity with men for college study.

Racial Background

A question relating to racial background was available in all thirteen CIRP years. The number of white adult freshmen fell from 87 percent in 1966 to 63 percent in 1975, and has remained around 70 percent since then (see table 2-8). In all thirteen years approximately 90 percent of the first-time, full-time freshmen were white. Black adult freshmen slightly outnumbered other adult minorities in postsecondary educational institutions—the Mexican-American/Chicano and Puerto Rican American racial groups were not distinguished from the other minority groups in the years 1966-70—but all of the minority groups increased their educational participation by 1978.

Table 2-8 also shows the ratios of the proportion of whites to all adults to the proportion of whites to all traditional students. If the ratio were 1.0 the same proportion of minorities would exist in the traditional and the adult student pools. Figures of less than 1.0 indicate that the proportion of minorities was higher in the adult student group. The highest ratio was .956 in 1966; it declined to .719 in 1974 and reached .806 in 1978. The trend in the ratio over time indicates that minorities became an increasingly important part of the pool of adults in college as opposed to their representation in the traditional-age student group. This trend was strongest from 1966 to 1974.

Bishop and Van Dyk (1977) have pointed out that participation in postsecondary education by minority-group members is much greater in metropolitan areas where college tuitions are relatively low. It may be that the growing representation of minorities in the CIRP adult population resulted from an increasing participation in the survey of two-year institu-

Table 2-7
Institutional Type and Enrollment Status of Adult Respondents, by Year and Sex
(*in percentages*)

	1972		1973		1974		1975		1976		1977		1978	
	M	F	M	F	M	F	M	F	M	F	M	F	M	F
All two-year colleges														
Part-time	21	40	25	40	30	43	26	37	18	29	21	30	23	30
Full-time	79	60	75	60	70	57	74	63	82	71	79	70	77	70
All four-year colleges														
Part-time	12	18	8	24	10	24	12	26	11	22	12	26	13	27
Full-time	87	82	92	76	90	76	88	74	89	78	88	74	87	73
All universities														
Part-time	13	30	10	27	10	20	10	20	11	23	9	21	8	17
Full-time	87	70	90	73	90	80	90	80	89	77	91	79	92	83
Predominantly black colleges														
Part-time	5	13	13	20	18	21	15	25	2	6	13	16	20	29
Full-time	95	87	87	80	82	80	85	75	98	94	87	84	80	71
All institutions														
Part-time	16	32	17	32	20	34	18	30	14	25	15	26	16	27
Full-time	84	68	83	68	80	66	82	70	86	75	85	74	84	73

Data unavailable for the years prior to 1972.
M = males, F = females.

Table 2-8
Race for All Institutions, by Year and Student Type (Traditional and Adult)
(in percentages)

| | Race | | | White Ratio[a] |
	White	Black	Other	
1966				
Traditional	91	5	5	.956
Adult	87	8	5	
1967				
Traditional	90	4	6	.944
Adult	85	9	7	
1968				
Traditional	87	6	7	.942
Adult	82	10	8	
1969				
Traditional	91	6	3	.923
Adult	84	11	5	
1970				
Traditional	89	9	2	.842
Adult	75	18	7	
1971				
Traditional	91	6	4	.835
Adult	76	15	9	
1972				
Traditional	87	9	7	.804
Adult	70	19	12	
1973				
Traditional	88	8	5	.750
Adult	66	24	11	
1974				
Traditional	89	7	7	.719
Adult	64	23	14	
1975				
Traditional	86	9	8	.732
Adult	63	25	12	
1976				
Traditional	86	8	7	.813
Adult	70	17	13	
1977				
Traditional	87	9	6	.780
Adult	68	20	13	
1978				
Traditional	88	8	6	.806
Adult	71	17	13	

[a]Ratio equals the proportion of white adults to all adult students divided by the proportion of white norms participants to all students in the norms.

tions, which have more minorities than do four-year institutions. Table 2-9 indicates that growth over time of the proportion of two-year college adults who were minority-group members closely parallels the growth of minority adults in the total sample. That is, the increased representation of minority adults reflects growth in both the two- and four-year sectors, not just a shift in sample composition toward increased participation of two-year colleges.

Table 2-10 describes the racial backgrounds of adult and traditional-age students of both sexes and for all institutions. In the earlier years for which data are available, a higher proportion of the adult women than adult men were black. In more recent years, about equal proportions of women and men were white but the proportion of black women was still higher than the proportion of black men. Whereas the proportions of men and women who fell into the "other" racial category were approximately equal in the early years, in the later years the proportion of women who were of "other" races became smaller than the proportion of men in this category. However the overall increase in the proportion of adult students of both sexes who were not white is substantial.

A much higher proportion of adults of both sexes were nonwhites as compared with traditional-age students (see tables 2-9 and 2-10). And the growth of nonwhite representation was much more rapid among the adults than among the traditional-age students.

Also evident from table 2-9 is that the proportion of white adults declined, perhaps a bit more so for women. The proportion of black women rose more than that of black men, particularly in recent years. More detailed trends by sex are revealed in table 2-9, but racial differences far outweighed changes by sex or institutional type over time.

From our data there does not seem to be much difference by race in the proportion of adults who are part- or full-time (see table 2-11). Roughly three times as many adults in the CIRP sample attended full time as attended part time in 1974. For all three racial categories, the proportion of full-timers increased by 1978, with a slightly larger increase for nonwhite adults. Efforts to remove barriers facing adults in higher education, such as providing sufficient financial aid, probably made it easier for them to attend full time in the later years, although the full-time proportion in the CIRP exceeded the real figure by a significant amount. The percentages attending part- or full-time were about the same for each racial category.

Marital Status

In the years after 1970 fewer married than unmarried adults usually attended college. For example, in 1971, 47 percent of the adult students were

Table 2-9

Race of Adult Respondents, for Institutional Type, by Sex and Year

(in percentages)

	All Two-Year Colleges			All Four-Year Colleges			All Universities			Predominantly Black Colleges		
	W	*B*	*O*	*W*	*B*	*O*	*W*	*B*	*O*	*W*	*B*	*O*
1966												
Men	85	10	6	93	2	6	94	2	4	7	82	10
Women	89	5	7	89	8	3	95	2	4	10	84	7
1967												
Men	85	8	6	89	4	7	92	3	6	5	86	9
Women	74	18	8	84	6	11	90	4	6	6	93	2
1968												
Men	83	10	7	89	4	6	92	3	5	9	68	13
Women	68	22	9	87	3	11	87	6	7	16	81	4
1969												
Men	85	8	6	88	7	5	93	5	2	10	81	9
Women	75	18	6	84	10	6	86	9	4	25	71	5
1970												
Men	80	13	7	82	11	7	88	6	6	12	86	1
Women	68	25	8	65	25	10	80	16	4	9	90	1
1971												
Men	77	11	10	85	8	6	87	5	8	12	78	10
Women	75	17	7	74	18	9	81	14	4	13	83	4
1972												
Men	71	14	16	76	15	12	85	8	10	5	84	11
Women	67	21	12	63	25	12	80	14	7	9	87	4
1973												
Men	66	22	11	76	13	11	86	7	8	5	90	5
Women	63	26	12	70	20	9	82	11	9	8	88	3
1974												
Men	61	22	18	75	14	13	80	9	13	8	82	8
Women	59	27	14	75	15	11	80	11	8	7	86	8
1975												
Men	62	24	13	73	13	14	79	9	13	10	79	12
Women	62	27	10	72	16	13	78	14	8	8	85	6
1976												
Men	72	14	16	75	12	16	77	12	14	14	70	16
Women	72	16	12	71	18	12	75	18	6	16	79	6
1977												
Men	70	12	17	73	13	16	81	9	12	6	78	16
Women	74	14	11	71	20	12	78	13	10	5	90	4
1978												
Men	78	10	14	73	11	16	79	7	13	8	68	29
Women	81	10	9	73	17	10	77	14	10	8	80	11

W = white, B = black, O = other.

Table 2-10

Race for All Institutions, by Year, Sex, and Student Type (Traditional and Adult)

(in percentages)

	White		Black		Other	
	T	A	T	A	T	A
1966						
Males	91	89	4	6	4	5
Females	83	90	11	6	6	5
1967						
Males	90	87	4	7	6	6
Females	90	80	5	12	6	7
1968						
Males	88	85	5	8	7	7
Females	86	76	7	15	7	9
1969						
Males	92	86	5	9	3	5
Females	90	79	7	15	3	6
1970						
Males	90	79	8	15	2	7
Females	87	66	11	26	2	7
1971						
Males	—	78	—	13	—	8
Females	—	73	—	20	—	7
1972						
Males	88	72	8	16	7	12
Females	86	66	10	23	7	10
1973						
Males	89	67	7	23	5	10
Females	88	64	9	26	5	9
1974						
Males	89	64	8	22	8	16
Females	88	63	8	25	6	13
1975						
Males	87	63	8	24	8	12
Females	86	63	10	26	7	9
1976						
Males	87	71	7	15	8	15
Females	85	70	10	20	7	11
1977						
Males	88	68	8	18	6	15
Females	86	68	10	22	6	11
1978						
Males	89	69	7	16	6	16
Females	88	72	9	19	6	9

T = CIRP norms participants, A = adult participants.

Table 2-11
Enrollment Status of Adult Respondents, by Year and Race
(in percentages)

	1974		1975	
Race	*Part-time*	*Full-time*	*Part-time*	*Full-time*
White	27	73	23	77
Black	26	74	20	80
Other	25	75	19	81

married; the percentage rose to 51 percent in 1975 but then fell steadily to 42 percent in 1978. Between 97 and 100 percent of the traditional-age students were unmarried. The extra responsibilities and greater financial and time restrictions of married people probably limit their ability to attend college. Of course we do not know whether married adults are more likely than single adults to have attended college previously, but if this is the case, lower attendance rates by married people might be due to more than the barriers they face.

Questions regarding whether respondents were separated, divorced, or widowed were not available on the CIRP questionnaires. So we divided the group of married adult students into those who were living with their spouses and those who were not. The separated, divorced, or widowed group thus fell into the second category along with the few married couples who, for example, might have separated to pursue careers in different geographical locations.

Table 2-12 indicates that more unmarried men than unmarried women and more women than men who were married and not living with their spouses attended postsecondary institutions in both 1975 and 1978. Many women who were married but not living with their spouses may have found themselves with few resources and inadequate skills with which to get a job to support themselves. Education may have been looked upon as a means to obtain the skills necessary for employment. We shall see that job-related concerns in decisions about attending college were more important for women not living with their spouses than for others. In 1975 there were equal numbers of adult men and women students who were married and living with their spouses, but by 1978 there were more women than men in this category. This probably reflects improved child-care services and changing attitudes in society toward single women participating in educational and vocational activities.

In both 1975 and 1978 the majority of the part-time adult student group were married and living with their spouses. This was especially true for men in 1975 (64 percent men versus 59 percent women) and for women in 1978 (57 percent women versus 50 percent men). The majority of the full-time

Table 2-12
Characteristics of Adult Respondents, by Marital Status
(in percentages)

	1975			1978		
	Unmarried	*Married, Living with Spouse*	*Married, Not Living with Spouse*	*Unmarried*	*Married, Living with Spouse*	*Married, Not Living with Spouse*
Sex						
Males	52	44	5	66	30	4
Females	45	44	11	51	40	9
Enrollment status						
Part-time	32	61	7	40	55	5
Full-time	54	38	8	63	30	9
Institutional type						
All two-year colleges	41	50	9	49	45	6
All four-year colleges	53	41	6	61	33	6
All universities	58	37	5	68	28	4
All black colleges	55	32	13	66	21	13
Race						
White	48	48	4	55	40	4
Black	48	36	16	63	22	15
Other	55	36	10	66	27	8

student group was unmarried adults. Also, there were more adults who were married but not living with their spouses in the full-time group than in the part-time group. It is obvious from these findings that most single adults and married adults not living with their spouses have fewer family-related responsibilities to infringe on the time they have to spend pursuing an education full time.

Two-year college enrollment primarily consisted of adults who were married and living with their spouses in 1975, but by 1978, there were slightly more unmarried adult males in two-year colleges (57 percent men versus 44 percent women). Unmarried adults were the majority in all other kinds of institutions. However in 1975 there were more women who were married and living with their spouses in four-year colleges than unmarried women (55 percent married women versus 46 percent unmarried women). It is surprising that in all institutions, enrollment of those who were married and living with their spouses dropped substantially by 1978. Black colleges enrolled the highest proportion of those who were married but not living with their spouses and universities enrolled the lowest.

There was a higher percentage of unmarried than married adults in all the racial groups examined. The white adult college population had the most respondents who were married and living with their spouses, and the black group had the most adults who were married but not living with their spouses. Slight differences do emerge when marital status by racial background is examined by sex. In 1975 the white and black racial groups had equal numbers of men who were married and living with their spouses (45 percent) and in the white group there were more women who were married and living with their spouses than unmarried women (52 percent married versus 42 percent unmarried).

Number of Children

In 1973, 81 percent of men aged 22 to 25 and 68 percent of women in the same age group had no children. For those 26 and over, 38 percent of the men and 20 percent of the women had no children. By 1976, 85 percent of the men aged 22 to 25 and 68 percent of the women had no children, while 43 percent of the older men and 21 percent of the older women did not have children. Of those who did have children, women (probably including many who were separated, divorced, or widowed) had more children than men regardless of their ages.

Father's and Mother's Educational Attainment

There is a big difference between the traditional-age students and the adults in the educational backgrounds of their parents. Across all years, the fathers and mothers of the traditional-age students were much more likely than those of the adults to have had at least some education beyond high school. Full-time adults generally had more educated parents than did part-time students in both 1974 and 1978. This might reflect higher incomes of full-time adult students, who are better able than part-timers to forego a full-time income. It is unclear however why the adults from more educated families did not attend college during the traditional college-going years. Perhaps they did attend then and returned later as a leisure activity.

According to the reasoning of the human capital theorists, the father's education will reflect a person's socioeconomic status (SES) because men have traditionally been more likely than women to be in the labor force and there is a positive correlation between education and income; the mother's education will reflect a child's at-home acquisition of human capital. On both counts, our sample reveals adult students to be disadvantaged compared with traditional-age students. Between 1966 and 1978, the proportion of adult students whose fathers had at least some postsecondary education rose from 25 to 31 percent, whereas for traditional students the proportion rose from 46 to 54 percent. This is another indication of the lower SES of adults. Over the same period the proportion of mothers of adults with at least some postsecondary education rose from 20 to 28 percent; for traditional students there was also an increase in the proportion of mothers who had attended college (from 38 to 45 percent).

Because the parents of adult students are older than the parents of younger students, these findings are not surprising, given the increasing educational attainments of the U.S. population. Nevertheless, traditional students are almost twice as likely as adult students to derive whatever benefits accrue to those coming from homes with educated parents. The challenge to the colleges to make up for these disadvantages is clear.

The adults who attend college seem to come from three pools. Some scholars believe that it is the high-SES adult who is likely to return to college—perhaps to take a variety of courses for enjoyment. Others believe in a "compensation" model—that those who were unable to move directly from high school into college (perhaps because of income pressures or low grades) return later to make up for what they missed earlier. Still others believe that adult participation in higher education is not entirely due to either the leisure or compensation models but that adults go or return to college because they want to update their skills. Perhaps their pattern of attendance is different from the traditional one. Their attendance is more sporadic or periodic with enrollments in degree programs not so much dictated by choice as by circumstance: Sporadic or periodic enrollment may be the only available option if adults are to study what they want. So our sample may include large groups of people who have periodically taken specific courses just to acquire skills or learn particular things but who must enroll in degree programs.

Although all of these hypotheses may be valid, one hypothesis should not be chosen instead of the others because the group of adult students is not a monolithic group. The data we have presented, indicating that adults come from lower-SES homes, lead us to prefer the compensation hypothesis. Hence, we conclude that adults will prefer colleges offering traditional, or at least career-related, programs to colleges catering to the leisure needs of affluent adults.

3 College Choice

Types of Institutions Attended as Freshmen

Schlaver (1977) has pointed out that large institutions enroll more students of different ages than small institutions do, but that most adults choose smaller, public colleges with lower admissions standards. That is, most adults attend two-year colleges while most traditional-age students attend four-year colleges. This difference in choice could be influenced by the kinds of courses offered at different institutions, lower tuition at two-year colleges, or geographical considerations. Anderson and Darkenwald (1979) have said that "geographical access or proximity to organizations that provide adult education has direct positive effect on participation rates" (p. 4).

The data in table 3-1 are consistent with this observation. The greatest concentration of adults exists in the two-year colleges, particularly those that are publicly controlled. Roughly 36 percent of the adult students were in two-year colleges in 1966 and 1978, but between these years, two-year college attendance rose to 64 percent in 1970 and then began to decline. There was a constant increase of adults in public four-year colleges (from 8 to 16 percent) and in private four-year colleges (from 3 to 8 percent). Catholic college attendance by adults also grew from 1 to 5 percent over the period. It is unclear why adult attendance at public universities declined so dramatically (from 40 to 15 percent) during the period covered. One possible explanation is that the absolute number of adults attending public universities remained stable and that all the growth took place in the two-year schools. The proportion of adults in Protestant colleges and private universities remained at about 4 and 5 percent respectively between 1966 and 1978.

Traditional-age students were distributed across institutions quite differently from adults. There has been a steady growth in the popularity of two-year colleges as attendance by traditional-age students has risen from 25 to 37 percent. Public four-year colleges have always had a greater proportion of younger than older students, and for the younger group that proportion has risen from 18 to 22 percent. Roughly equal numbers of traditional and adult students attended private four-year colleges in 1978 (about 8 percent), although the proportion of traditional-age students had remained constant while the adult proportion had risen. The traditional-age

Table 3-1
Adult and Traditional Students in Postsecondary Education, by Year and Type of Institution
(in percentages)

	1966		1967		1968		1969		1970		1971	
	T	A	T	A	T	A	T	A	T	A	T	A
All two-year colleges	25	36	31	44	30	44	36	49	36	64	39	52
All four-year colleges	45	16	43	14	40	18	37	19	40	18	38	22
All universities	30	46	26	39	29	35	28	29	25	14	23	21
Predominantly black colleges	—	3	—	2	—	3	—	2	—	4	2	5
Two-year colleges (public)	20	30	25	38	24	39	27	42	28	59	36	47
Two-year colleges (private)	5	5	5	5	6	4	9	6	7	5	4	4
Technical institutions	—	1	—	1	—	2	—	1	—	1	3	1
Four-year colleges (public)	18	8	15	7	21	9	19	10	21	9	19	10
Four-year colleges (private)	7	3	7	3	7	3	7	4	7	4	6	5
Four-year colleges (Protestant)	11	4	12	3	6	4	6	3	6	3	6	4
Four-year colleges (Catholic)	6	1	7	1	4	2	3	2	3	2	3	4
Universities (public)	23	40	19	35	24	30	22	25	17	11	18	16
Universities (private)	7	4	7	4	6	5	5	4	7	3	5	4
Predominantly black institutions (public)	—	2	—	1	—	1	—	1	—	3	—	4
Predominantly black institutions (private)	—	1	—	1	—	2	—	2	—	1	—	1

	T	A	T	A	T	A	T	A	T	A	T	A	T	A
All two-year colleges	39	51	41	49	41	53	42	46	44	42	40	43	37	37
All four-year colleges	38	22	36	24	35	22	35	24	34	31	38	30	38	34
All universities	23	22	23	19	24	19	23	21	22	22	23	19	25	20
Predominantly black colleges	—	5	2	8	2	6	3	9	3	5	3	8	3	9
Two-year colleges (public)	35	48	38	45	38	50	39	42	41	38	37	40	34	34
Two-year colleges (private)	4	3	3	4	3	3	3	4	3	4	3	3	4	3
Technical institutions	—	—	—	—	—	—	—	—	—	—	—	—	—	—
Four-year colleges (public)	19	12	20	13	20	11	10	14	19	18	22	16	22	16
Four-year colleges (private)	7	5	7	5	7	4	7	3	7	6	7	6	7	8
Four-year colleges (Protestant)	6	3	6	3	6	4	6	3	6	3	5	4	6	4
Four-year colleges (Catholic)	3	2	3	2	3	2	3	3	3	4	3	4	3	5
Universities (public)	18	18	18	15	19	16	18	17	17	18	18	15	19	15
Universities (private)	5	4	5	4	5	4	5	4	5	5	5	4	6	6
Predominantly black institutions (public)	—	2	—	7	—	5	—	7	—	5	—	7	—	6
Predominantly black institutions (private)	—	2	—	1	—	1	—	1	—	1	—	1	—	3

T = CIRP norms participants, A = adult participants.

students in religiously controlled colleges declined over the period. The proportion of traditional students in public universities declined, but not as much as the proportion of adult students.

To summarize, the number of traditional-age students in two-year colleges rose so that by 1978 the same proportion of adults and traditional students attended. However, it is likely that many part-time adults in two-year colleges were not identified in the CIRP sample. Although over the years the proportion of traditional students in four-year colleges declined, while the proportion of adults rose, a smaller number of adults still attended four-year colleges. At the university level a slightly higher proportion of traditional than adult students attended.

From 1974 through 1978, respondents were asked whether the college in which they enrolled was their first choice, second choice, and so on. The majority of both traditional-age (75 percent) and adult students (84 to 90 percent) attended their first-choice colleges as freshmen, while fewer than 20 percent attended institutions that were not their first choice (see table 3-2). There was virtually no difference between part-time and full-time adults in the probability of attending their first-choice institutions. This would be surprising if adult and traditional students applied to the same institutions, given the poorer preparation by the adults. However, except for 1976 and 1978, a higher proportion of adult than younger students enrolled

Table 3-2
Choice of College for All Institutions, by Year and Student Type (Traditional and Adult)
(in percentages)

	Less than Second Choice	Second Choice	First Choice
1974			
Traditional	6	19	76
Adult	4	12	84
1975			
Traditional	5	17	78
Adult	4	10	87
1976			
Traditional	6	17	77
Adult	4	10	86
1977			
Traditional	6	19	75
Adult	3	11	86
1978			
Traditional	6	18	76
Adult	3	10	90

Data unavailable for the years prior to 1974.

in two-year colleges. Moreover, adults who attended four-year institutions were usually enrolled in less selective schools than were traditional students.

Students can improve their chances of being accepted to their first-choice institution by applying only to colleges that do not have stringent admissions requirements. Twenty-four percent of the adults applied to one nonselective four-year college and no others, whereas only 18 percent of traditional students did this. This in part explains why more adults attended their first-choice institutions. Traditional students were more likely to apply to more institutions than were adults. Adults probably applied to more local institutions because their restricted mobility limited their choices. Thus adults were probably more likely to attend their first-choice colleges because their first-choice colleges had less stringent admissions requirements than the colleges preferred by traditional students. As we shall see, other factors (immobility, financial constraints, need to work part time) limit the choice for many adults to two-year or other nonselective local institutions. Also, younger students might apply to "riskier" colleges (which they prefer but have little chance of being admitted to) on the chance that they might get admitted.

**Why College Students Selected the
College They Attended**

In each survey year except 1966, 1969, 1970, and 1971, CIRP freshmen were asked about their reasons for selecting the college they attended. As shown in table 3-3, the primary reason given by adults (and even more frequently by traditional students) was that the college had a good academic reputation. This is surprising because adults most often attended two-year colleges, which are not generally considered academically superior to other types of colleges. In fact, it is generally believed that adjunct faculty, who may be less qualified academically than regular faculty, teach adult college students in two-year colleges. Hence for 1978 freshmen, responses were broken down in table 3-4 by type of institution attended. The frequency of this reason still stands out. Academic reputation was by far the most popular reason given by adult and traditional students. Fewer of both groups in the two-year colleges (38 percent) indicated that their choice was based on academic reputation, and for the adult group in this sector, reputation was less important than the fact that the selected two-year colleges offered special educational programs (indicated by 41 percent). Only in 1975, when the reason "it will help to get a better job" was suggested, did academic reputation rank below the top (66 percent of the adults and 51 percent of the younger students selected the job-related reason for their choice). It is unfortunate that this reason was not included in the survey in

Table 3-3
Reasons Noted as "Very Important" in Selecting this College, for All Institutions, by Year and Student Type (Traditional and Adult)
(in percentages)

	1967		1968		1972		1973		1974		1975		1976		1977		1978	
	T	A	T	A	T	A	T	A	T	A	T	A	T	A	T	A	T	A
Relatives wanted me to come here	46	23	48	24	10	5	9	4	8	6	8	6	7	4	6	4	6	4
Teacher advised me	—	—	—	—	—	—	5	4	5	5	5	3	4	3	4	4	4	3
Has a good academic reputation	46	34	43	31	48	43	49	44	50	50	48	46	43	40	48	47	51	47
Offered financial assistance	—	—	—	—	18	18	17	23	19	24	17	19	14	17	15	19	14	18
Not accepted anywhere else	—	—	—	—	3	2	—	—	—	—	—	—	3	2	3	2	3	2
Advice of someone who attended	—	—	—	—	17	16	19	19	18	20	17	19	14	16	16	18	14	16
Offers special educational programs	—	—	—	—	27	39	29	43	30	48	28	43	25	38	29	40	26	38
Has low tuition	22	26	25	24	20	24	27	35	28	36	25	33	18	23	18	24	17	21
Advice of guidance counselor	—	—	—	—	7	6	10	7	9	8	8	6	8	5	8	5	8	5
Wanted to live at home	—	—	—	—	13	22	14	23	13	26	14	23	12	23	12	24	10	24
Friend suggested attending	—	—	—	—	—	—	—	—	—	—	7	12	7	11	8	12	9	11
College representative recruited me	13	10	12	10	—	—	—	—	—	—	4	2	4	2	4	3	4	3
Could not get a job	—	—	—	—	—	—	3	8	3	10	4	9	—	—	—	—	—	—
Wanted to live away from home	16	2	15	3	18	4	15	4	14	4	14	4	—	—	—	—	—	—
It will help to get a better job	—	—	—	—	—	—	—	—	—	—	51	66	—	—	—	—	—	—
Has a good athletic program	6	2	6	2	10	5	—	—	—	—	—	—	—	—	—	—	—	—
Most friends going here	—	—	—	—	4	2	—	—	—	—	—	—	—	—	—	—	—	—

T = CIRP norms participants, A = adult participants.
Data unavailable for the following years: 1966, 1969, 1970, 1971.

Table 3-4

Reasons Noted as "Very Important" in Selecting Type of College, for 1978 (Traditional and Adult)

(in percentages)

Reasons	All Two-Year Colleges		All Four-Year Colleges		All Universities		Predominantly Black Colleges	
	T	A	T	A	T	A	T	A
Relatives wanted me to come here	6	4	6	4	5	3	11	11
Teacher advised me	4	2	4	4	3	4	7	6
Has a good academic reputation	38	38	55	52	63	55	50	41
Offered financial assistance	11	16	19	19	13	16	28	21
Not accepted anywhere else	4	2	2	2	2	1	3	2
Advice of someone who attended	13	15	15	17	13	14	16	23
Offers special educational programs	24	41	27	38	26	34	32	38
Has low tuition	21	29	14	13	14	14	19	39
Advice of guidance counselor	9	5	7	5	6	3	10	7
Wanted to live at home	15	29	9	22	4	19	10	21
Friend suggested attending	6	11	7	12	6	8	8	14
College representative recruited me	3	2	7	3	3	1	10	6

T = CIRP norms participants, A = adult participants.

all of the years examined because in most of the literature, job-related reasons were the most frequently mentioned by adults for either beginning to attend or returning to institutions of postsecondary education.

It seems that those who until recently did not have a chance to participate in higher education, particularly women, were the ones who most frequently gave "increasing chance of achieving job-related aspirations" as a reason for attending college (Bishop and Van Dyk 1977; Gibson 1977). Our data show that in 1975 married women, especially those who were not living with their spouses, were more likely to give job-related reasons for attending college than men (see tables A-1 and A-2). Also "low tuition" and "offered financial assistance" were much more important reasons for attending college for unmarried women and married women who were not living with their spouses. Financial concerns of women in all marital groups seemed to decrease by 1978, as fewer women gave financial reasons for choosing a particular college. This is probably because as more and more women entered the labor force they were better able to pay for their educations.

Those with no more than a high-school education, who dropped out to get married or take jobs, or because going to college was not a standard in their neighborhoods, also gave job-related reasons because they felt that more education would improve their chances of moving into a new job. Adults with more education are generally in professional white-collar jobs already and merely seek improvement or advancement at their present jobs (Arbeiter 1977; Harrington 1977).

Some believe that education is a much more important means of mobility today than it has been in the past. Surely, as more and more people obtain college degrees, the cost of not having one grows. Some people who are unemployed return to school to increase their opportunities for employment. London, Wenkert, and Hagstrom (1963) point out that the incidence of psychological breakdown increases when unemployment rates are high and that further education can be therapeutic.

Adults who seek midlife career changes indicate that job-related aspirations are their reasons for attending college (O'Keefe 1977). They want to acquire the new skills needed to make a transition.

Another job-related reason adults give for attending college concerns their present jobs (Indiana Commission for Higher Education 1979). As we mentioned earlier, most of the adults who give this reason have more education than other adults and are already employed in professional white-collar jobs. These people, who want to improve their performance at their present jobs, are more interested in being trained than in receiving an education (Gibson 1977). Also, additional study is increasingly becoming a requirement for the retention of professional licenses (Harrington 1977). Many adults enter educational institutions to acquire flexible skills in a rapidly changing, technological society (Kyle 1979; O'Keefe 1977). The question arises: Will adults enroll or reenroll in college for career-related training or will the need for this kind of training cause them to choose extension, short-term, or in-house, on-the-job training programs rather than traditional colleges?

The dominance of academic reputation, both over time and across institutional types, might be explained in several ways. Students may be comparing their institutions not with Harvard, but rather with nearby colleges with poor reputations. Or the interpretation of "good academic reputation" may be different from the interpretation used in national ranking studies: A school friends attended might be viewed as academically sound regardless of what the friends learned there, or a two-year college known to have a fine program in auto repair might be viewed as having a good academic reputation.

Other reasons adult students gave for selecting a particular college were: the college offered special educational programs (38 to 48 percent, depending upon the year), the college had a low tuition (23 to 36 percent), the students wanted to live at home (about 25 percent), and the students were offered financial assistance (about 20 percent) (see table 3-3). The importance of special educational programs is particularly interesting, but again the significance of this reason is unclear. The special program that is attractive might be one in auto repair or in the humanities, or it might be a remedial or counseling program that facilitates the entry and progress of adults. But most special programs are probably occupationally oriented.

Reasons that were least important to adults in selecting a particular college included not being accepted anywhere else or wanting to live away from home.

The younger students had similar reasons for selecting a particular college. In 1967 and 1968 however the most important reason for selecting a particular college was that their relatives wanted them to attend that college. Another important reason for younger students was to live away from home.

In 1978 low tuition was particularly important in two-year and predominantly black institutions. This reason for attending a particular college was more important to adults than younger students. It is clear that programmatic and financial considerations are very important when adults select their colleges. Adults were more likely than younger students to have attended because they were unemployed (about 9 percent said not being able to get a job was a very important reason, compared with about 3 percent of traditional students). Few adults were influenced by relatives, teachers, counselors, or college recruiters.

Research on participation shows the importance of word-of-mouth and friends in selecting a particular college. Friends provide a sense of personal relevance and legitimacy missing from impersonal program announcements. Yet, it seems that more information must be made available to adults if in fact they are misinformed about available options, the academic reputations and programmatic offerings of these options, and how to secure financial aid at institutions other than those with very low tuition. More effective recruiting, along with dissemination of information, could probably attract some adults to colleges they have not considered in the past. But word-of-mouth will probably always be an important factor in college choice.

With several notable exceptions, table 3-5 reveals that adults, regardless of enrollment status, had similar reasons for selecting their colleges in 1974 and 1978. Part-timers were less inclined to indicate "good academic reputation" as a reason. Part-time adults, particularly those who are working, would not be as free to move in order to attend an institution with a good reputation. Nevertheless, even among part-timers, almost 40 percent did indicate this reason.

Table 3-5
Reasons Noted as "Very Important" in Selecting this Particular College, for Adult Respondents, by Enrollment Status and Year
(in percentages)

	1974		1978	
	Part-time	Full-time	Part-time	Full-time
My relatives wanted me to come here	5	6	4	4
I wanted to live away from home	2	4	—	—
My teacher advised me	4	5	2	4
This college has a very good academic reputation	39	53	37	49
I was offered financial assistance	15	28	9	20
Someone who had been here before advised me to go	20	20	15	16
This college offers special educational programs	48	48	32	39
This college has low tuition	42	34	25	20
My guidance counselor advised me	8	8	4	5
I wanted to live at home	33	23	35	21
I could not get a job	7	11	—	—
I was not accepted anywhere else	—	—	1	2
A friend suggested attending	—	—	12	10
A college representative recruited me	—	—	2	3

Offers of financial aid appeared to be more important reasons for selecting a particular college for full-time adults, while low tuition was a more important reason for part-time adults. Clearly only full-timers are likely to qualify for aid. Finally, the desire to live at home was more important for part-timers. This is probably attributable to a number of factors, especially job and family responsibilities and financial considerations.

Regardless of whether adult choices of colleges are based upon adequate and accurate information, several things are clear. Adults select colleges that they perceive to be of high quality and that offer job-related training, and they seek low-cost options. Research suggests that more and more four-year colleges are offering occupational programs as part of their curriculum. "A constant in the history of higher education in this country has been the changing nature of the curriculum. Today, the curriculum is still changing but these changes may now be as much a result of internal as of external pressures. One external pressure is to make the curriculum more sensitive to the occupational life of the institution's graduates; one internal pressure is the desire to survive." (Campbell and Korim 1979, foreword). Nevertheless, there does not seem to be much evidence in our data that the adults in college are the wealthy, attending school to fill their leisure hours. Yet differences between part-time and full-time adult students should be noted.

4 Financing of College Education

Financial considerations are critical for adults returning to college. Inability to finance a college education can have several effects. As Leslie (1978) has noted, the lack of financial resources to meet the cost of instruction is both prohibiting and limiting. If financial concerns are great enough during the time when a potential student is deciding whether to attend college, he may decide to forego college altogether or to select an urban institution with low tuition that is close to home (Shulman 1976). Once a student is in college, excessive financial worries may increase the probability of his dropping out before completing his program. Because the CIRP data represent only students already enrolled in the first year of college, those whose financial concerns were great enough to prevent them from attending are not included. Nevertheless, it is important to assess the extent to which adults enrolled in college express concern about their financial resources and to compare the concerns of adults with the concerns of traditional-age students. Some adults may be unaware of available resources. And some financial aid programs have stipulations that limit their accessibility to adults. So if adults do express concerns, it is important to determine what these concerns are so that action can be taken to alleviate them.

Most adult and traditional-age students expressed some concern about their financial situations but felt they would probably have enough money to cover their educational costs (see table 4-1). Of course, the concern reflected by CIRP respondents may seriously understate the concern in the adult population as a whole: those with the greatest concern probably did not attend college. Approximately equal numbers of adult and traditional-age students felt confident that they would have enough money for college in most of the years between 1966 and 1978. The proportion expressing this confidence was usually around 35 percent of both groups, although a slightly higher proportion of adults (37 to 41 percent) were confident in the 1972-74 period, a time when more adults were drawing on their GI Bill benefits, probably after serving in the Vietnam War. In those years, about 50 percent of the adults were receiving GI benefits, compared with 45 percent in 1966 (see table 4-2). Since the early 1970s the proportion of adults relying on GI benefits has declined dramatically, from a high of 58 percent in 1971 to 15 percent in 1978 (see tables 4-2 and 4-3). Clearly, alternative sources of support had to be found for adults. Judging from the fact that

Table 4-1
Financial Concerns of Respondents, for All Institutions, by Year and Student Type (Traditional and Adult)
(in percentages)

	None *("confident I will have sufficient funds")*	*Some Concern* *("but I will probably have enough funds")*	*Major Concern* *("not sure I will be able to complete college")*
1966			
Traditional	35	56	9
Adult	35	52	13
1967			
Traditional	34	57	9
Adult	38	51	12
1968			
Traditional	35	56	8
Adult	34	53	12
1969			
Traditional	34	56	10
Adult	34	52	15
1970			
Traditional	34	55	11
Adult	37	49	14
1971			
Traditional	34	56	10
Adult	35	51	14
1972			
Traditional	36	49	15
Adult	37	41	22
1973			
Traditional	36	48	17
Adult	37	38	25
1974			
Traditional	39	46	15
Adult	41	36	23
1975			
Traditional	37	47	16
Adult	36	38	26
1976			
Traditional	35	49	16
Adult	34	40	26
1977			
Traditional	34	49	17
Adult	32	41	27
1978			
Traditional	35	51	15
Adult	32	42	26

the decline in adults' confidence in their ability to pay tuition has been much smaller than the decline in use of GI benefits, some progress seems to have been made in this area.

However, the proportion of both groups of freshmen who expressed major concern about finances has risen during the period considered: from 9 to 15 percent for traditional-age students and from 13 to 26 percent for adult students (see table 4-1). A review of the literature suggests that these findings should not come as a surprise. As Schlaver (1977) says, "adults pay their own way whereas youth are subsidized" (p. 42). Whether adults are forced to finance their own educations because financial aid is not available to them is a more difficult question.

Financial concern by marital status was considered for the years 1975 and 1978 (see table A-3). Adult students who were married and living with their spouses were not as worried about financing their college educations as those who were married but not living with their spouses or those who were unmarried.

Also considered was the difference in financial concern between part-time and full-time adult students in 1974 and 1978 (see table A-4). Part-timers had significantly less concern than full-timers, probably because they could work while attending college. In 1974, 58 percent of the part-time but only 35 percent of the full-time adult students had no financial concerns. However by 1978 concern of both full-time and part-time adult students had increased. This difference is confirmed by the regressions that follow.

In each year, over 60 percent of the adults in college expressed at least some concern about their ability to finance their educations. To characterize further the adults who were most concerned with costs, multiple regressions were run for four of the thirteen adult freshman cohorts (1966, 1970, 1974, and 1978). The dependent variable was degree of concern about ability to finance their college educations (1 = none, 2 = some, 3 = major concern); the independent variables were type of institution attended, major, and a variety of demographic and socioeconomic traits, which unfortunately were not available in all years. The beta coefficients presented in table 4-4 represent statistically significant partial correlations (that is, correlations net of the effects of the other factors in the model). The fact that the multiple correlation coefficient (R^2) was very low for each regression tells us that factors not considered here are much more influential in determining financial concern than the ones that are considered here. For example, the highest proportion of variance in "concern" was accounted for in 1974, the only year for which a measure of personal (as distinct from parental) income was available. Clearly this is an important factor, yet even when it was included, only 15 percent of the variance was explained.

What is clear from the available data is that adults from poorer families, and black adults (even after holding income constant), had the most con-

Table 4-2

Source of Financing First Year of College, for All Institutions, by Year and Student Type (Traditional and Adult)

(in percentages)

	1966 T	1966 A	1967 T	1967 A	1968 T	1968 A	1969 T	1969 A	1973 T	1973 A	1974 T	1974 A	1975 T	1975 A	1976 T	1976 A	1977 T	1977 A	1978 T	1978 A
Parental, family aid, or gifts	—	—	—	—	—	—	—	—	80	24	80	23	80	22	56	18	80	26	72	18
Parental or other family aid	—	—	—	26	—	25	—	24	—	—	—	—	—	—	—	—	—	—	—	—
Parental aid	—	19	—	—	—	—	—	—	—	—	—	—	—	—	—	—	—	—	—	—
Grants or scholarships																				
Scholarship, grant, or other gift	—	—	—	31	—	35	—	38	—	—	—	—	—	—	—	—	—	—	—	—
Scholarship and grants	—	—	—	—	—	—	—	—	40	30	—	—	—	—	—	—	—	—	—	—
Scholarship	7	—	—	—	—	—	—	—	—	—	—	—	—	—	—	—	—	—	—	—
Basic Educational Opportunity Grant	—	—	—	—	—	—	—	—	—	—	25	22	27	23	21	24	33	41	22	25
Supplemental Ed Opportunity Grant	—	—	—	—	—	—	—	—	—	—	6	8	6	12	5	6	9	13	6	7
College work-study grant	—	—	—	—	—	—	—	—	—	—	13	11	12	9	9	7	16	15	11	8
State scholarship or grant	—	—	—	—	—	—	—	—	—	—	19	11	15	11	13	8	21	17	15	12
College grant (other than above)	—	—	—	—	—	—	—	—	—	—	—	—	—	—	9	5	17	12	12	8
Local or private scholarship or grant	—	—	—	—	—	—	—	—	—	—	20	8	18	6	—	—	—	—	—	—
Other private grant	—	—	—	—	—	—	—	—	—	—	—	—	—	—	6	3	10	6	7	3
Loans																				
Federally insured loans or college loans (for example, NDEA)	—	—	—	—	—	—	—	—	20	25	—	—	—	—	—	—	—	—	—	—
Federally guaranteed student loan	—	—	—	—	—	—	—	—	—	—	10	14	10	11	7	8	13	15	10	11
National direct student loan	—	—	—	—	—	—	—	—	—	—	9	8	10	8	7	5	11	10	8	7
Loan from the college	—	—	—	—	—	—	—	—	—	—	—	—	—	—	3	2	5	5	4	3
Tuition deferment loan from college	4	—	—	—	—	—	—	—	—	—	—	—	—	—	—	—	—	—	—	—
Repayable loan	—	—	—	16	—	18	—	19	—	—	—	—	—	—	—	—	—	—	—	—
Other repayable loan	—	—	—	—	—	—	—	—	8	9	—	—	—	—	—	—	—	—	—	—
Federal government	15	—	—	—	—	—	—	—	—	—	—	—	—	—	—	—	—	—	—	—
Commercial loan	5	—	—	—	—	—	—	—	—	—	—	—	—	—	—	—	—	—	—	—
Other loan	—	—	—	—	—	—	—	—	—	—	7	7	6	6	4	3	6	6	4	3

Work and Savings:

Part-time or summer work	—	—	—	—	—	—	—	—	—	—	73	52	70	43	64	37	50	26	68	45	—	—
Employment during summer	42	—	—	—	—	—	—	—	—	—	—	—	—	—	—	—	—	—	—	—	—	—
Other part-time work while attending college	—	—	—	—	—	—	—	—	—	—	—	—	—	—	—	—	—	—	—	—	25	23
Employment during college	48	—	—	—	—	—	—	—	—	—	—	—	—	—	—	—	—	—	—	—	—	—
Full-time work while attending college	—	—	—	—	—	—	—	—	—	—	12	38	11	35	9	28	6	15	8	30	2	15
Full-time work	—	—	—	—	—	—	72	—	71	—	—	—	—	—	—	—	—	—	—	—	—	16
Personal savings and/or employment	—	—	—	74	—	—	—	—	—	—	—	—	—	—	—	—	—	—	—	—	47	16
Savings from summer work	—	—	—	—	—	—	—	—	—	—	—	—	—	—	—	—	—	—	—	—	20	15
Personal savings	48	—	—	—	—	—	—	—	—	—	54	41	57	36	53	33	40	22	56	39	20	15
Spouse	—	—	—	—	—	—	—	—	—	—	3	34	2	29	2	25	1	15	2	26	1	16
GI Bill	45	—	—	—	—	—	—	—	—	—	—	—	—	—	—	—	—	—	—	—	—	—
GI benefits from your military service	—	—	—	—	—	—	—	—	—	—	2	52	2	41	2	39	1	20	1	28	1	15
Federal benefits from parent's military service	—	—	—	—	—	—	—	—	—	—	4	4	2	2	2	2	1	13	2	2	1	1
Parents' social security benefits	—	—	—	—	—	—	—	—	—	—	8	2	9	3	10	2	6	2	9	3	6	1
Other	—	—	—	—	—	—	—	—	—	—	6	13	6	11	6	11	8	6	6	12	4	6

T = CIRP norms participants, A = adult participants.

Data unavailable for the following years: 1970, 1971, 1972.

Table 4-3
Source of Financing College Education for Adult Respondents, for All Institutions, by Year
(in percentages)

	1970	1971	1972
Parental, family aid, or gifts	19	35	28
Scholarships and grants	12	23	33
NDEA loans, federally insured loans, or college loans	11	24	32
Other repayable loans	7	14	19
Part-time or summer work	45	64	65
Savings from full-time employment	38	54	54
Spouse's employment	—	—	42
Federal benefits from parent's military service	3	4	4
GI benefits from your military service	51	58	55

cern about money. Despite the fact that financial aid programs have been targeted for these groups, these programs have not alleviated financial concerns, at least among adult students. Because blacks are more highly represented in the adult college population than in the traditional-age group, perhaps a financial assistance program should be established for this group to make up for previous educational disadvantages.

Women and younger adults also displayed more financial concern. Because the coefficient on the sex variable was highest when independent income was included, it appears that the concerns of female adult students were independent of income. Few women have access to GI Bill benefits; many adult women have constrained mobility (less freedom to select the least expensive college); and many must attend part time due to household responsibilities (whereas men who attend part time may receive some subsidy from their employers). Thus, the special problems of adult women returning to college must be confronted directly. Among adults, increased age probably reflects increased earnings or savings, which explains the negative relationship between age and concern about finance.

In the 1978 regression, the unmarried adults had more financial concerns than the married adults did. However in 1974, when personal income was included, the sign on the marital status variable was reversed. This leads to the inference that holding income constant, married adults have more financial concerns than single adults, a finding that makes sense given the additional expenses associated with raising a family. The 1978 results probably reflect the fact that single adults have fewer resources (lower incomes) than married adults.

The most consistent correlations regarding type of institution attended and concern with ability to finance college revealed that adults attending public two-year colleges had the least concern and adults attending private

Table 4-4
Correlates with Concern about Ability to Finance College Education

	1966	1970	1974	1978
Black colleges		− .075		
Public two-year colleges		− .125	− .061	− .079
Public four-year colleges			.018	− .047
Private four-year colleges	.033		.028	
Protestant four-year colleges				
Catholic four-year colleges		− .030		.030
University, private	.044		.028	.033
Black, public			− .070	
Technical college	.033		*	*
Sex (2 = female)		.074	.113	.094
Age	*	− .091	− .046	− .040
Marital status (2 = married)	*		.070	− .055
White		− .090	− .106	
Black			.030	.061
Parental income	− .171	− .140	− .171	− .228
Mother's education	.035			
Own income	*	*	− .127	*
Agriculture	.042			
Biological Science			.019	.022
Business	− .033	− .046	− .058	− .069
Education		.028		
Engineering				− .038
Arts		.025		
Preprofessional	.041	.046		.023
Social science	.028			
Technical			− .029	− .036
Nontechnical				− .027
Full-time	*	*	.166	
Part-time	*	*		− .107
First-time, full-time	*	*	.115	− .026
R^2	.0334	.0606	.1565	.1147
N	5,157	6,615	12,361	8,866

Note: Variables never entering: College types (all two-year, all four-year, all university, private two-year, university public, black private); Other race; Major (English, health, history, humanities, mathematics, physical science, undecided); First-time, part-time.

1 = none; 2 = some; 3 = major.

Positive coefficient = > higher independent variable = more concern.

* = not available this year.

Blank = not significant.

universities or four-year colleges had the most. These effects hold both before and after controlling for race and socioeconomic background, as well as for personal income or proxies for income such as sex, age, and marital status. Hence, it appears that adults choose low-cost public two-year institutions partly to reduce their financial concerns, which seem to be present regardless of their income levels. If the regressions had revealed less financial concern for adults at the more expensive institutions, we might have concluded that the rich chose the more expensive institutions and their secure financial conditions had alleviated money worries, whereas the poor went to inexpensive institutions and still had financial concerns. But this was not the case. It follows then that financial aid should be made available to adult students (regardless of their income) to insure their access to more expensive (and, as some argue, better) institutions of higher education.

Controlling for the factors discussed above, business and technical majors consistently had the least concern for their ability to pay for college, whereas preprofessional and biological science majors had the most. Perhaps business and technical majors are more receptive to loan programs or, more likely, perhaps they already hold jobs and can thus afford to pay for their educations. Preprofessional majors' concerns probably reflect the fact that they anticipate many years of paying for advanced training. Other than the cases just noted, adults in different majors did not differ in their concerns about their ability to finance college.

We now return to data on how adults actually have paid for college over the years (see tables 4-3 and 4-4). Before looking at the detailed data that have been collected, a serious omission must be noted. Because the CIRP survey was aimed primarily at students who entered college directly from high school, little consideration was given to employer-financed ways of paying for college. So we have no data on tuition remission or paid educational leave programs. Some respondents may have included such sources of support under the employment category. And the sampling procedures probably excluded many adults using employer subsidies for higher education. Nevertheless, we must keep in mind that this method of financing education may become increasingly important in encouraging adults to return to college.

From 1966 to 1969 and from 1973 to 1978, a question regarding financing was available, phrased as "source of financing first year of college." Adult students in these years indicated that work and savings were important sources of financing first year educational expenses. This was true regardless of institutional type. All items in this category however decreased in importance over the years. GI benefits from their military service were used by adults in 1974, particularly by students in two-year colleges and blacks (see tables A-5, A-6, and A-7). The Basic Educational Opportunity Grant (BEOG) was a significant source of financing for blacks and other minorities, especially if they were in four-year colleges or universities. Those from minority groups, other than blacks, relied on parental aid as one major source of financing their college educations, particularly if they were attending four-year colleges in 1974 or if they were attending black colleges.

For traditional-age students from 1966 through 1969, only *major* sources of financial support during freshman year were available in the CIRP national norms publications. These students relied on some type of parental or family aid as their major sources of financing, and loans and the GI Bill were relied on least.

From 1973 on, the category of family aid was still by far the most important source of financing first-year educational expenses, and the categories of spouse and GI benefits (whether their own or their parents) were the least important.

From 1970 to 1972, the question was phrased a little differently: "source of financing college education" (not just the first year). For adults in these years the major source of financing their college educations was their own military benefits. Personal savings or employment were relied on by about one-third of the adult sample. Again, in these years the CIRP norms reported only major sources. Younger students had more limited sources of financial support than their adult counterparts. As in the other years, they counted on family and savings from part-time summer work to pay for their educations.

The CIRP data on adults reveal a number of other interesting trends as well. In the early years of the survey, slightly less than 25 percent of the adults used some form of loan to finance their college educations. By 1972, 32 percent had a National Defense Education Act Loan (NDEA) or college loan and 19 percent had another kind of repayable loan. Since 1973, as student loan programs grew, the number of adults holding "other" loans (not college-related) had declined dramatically to 3 percent. Yet the proportion holding Federally Guaranteed Student Loans (FGSL), National Direct Student Loans (NDSL), NDEA, or other college loans had not risen enough to offset this decline. Even if we assume that each individual from 1974 on held only one kind of college-related loan, only about 20 percent of the adults were taking advantage of educational loan programs. It is not clear whether this represents a change in attitudes toward loans or a feeling that commercial interest rates are unreasonable when subsidized loans are available.

It is generally acknowledged that the heyday of the loan programs has passed. Yet one would expect that adults, particularly those with some business experience, would be more receptive to this method of financing college than younger students. However as interest rates have risen since the mid-1970s, commercial loans are less desirable and it wasn't until 1979 that limits on earnings were removed from the subsidized educational loan programs. In the late 1970s, adult students faced high commercial lending rates and low limits on earnings to qualify for subsidized loans. Nevertheless, adults in college have either been more likely than younger students to accept loans or they have had fewer choices. Adults seem to be more willing to go into debt than younger students. Younger students are more likely to drop out of college because of the debt. Astin (1976) found that reliance on loans is associated with higher drop-out rates among men in all income groups but the effects of loans on women are highly variable depending on the amount of the loan and the income level of the women's parents. However the Astin study considered only traditional-age students.

Adults in our sample appeared to have reasonable access to grant or scholarship aid. In the late 1960s, 30-40 percent of the adults in the CIRP files received some sort of gift (nonreturnable) aid. Yet in the early 1970s the number of adults who received such aid fluctuated, but averaged somewhere in the 20-30 percent range. In the mid- and late 1970s, after the aid programs from the 1972 Higher Education Amendments took effect, about 25 percent of adults received BEOG grants, 10 percent Supplemental Educational Opportunity Grants (SEOG), 15 percent state scholarships, and another 10 percent some other kind of grant. According to our data, these percentages do not differ significantly from patterns revealed by traditional-age students.

There were significant differences in sources of educational financing between full- and part-time adult students (see table A-8). Full-timers were much more likely than part-timers to have had parental or family help, and were much more likely to have received public subsidy in the form of grants, loans, or work-study. Part-time students were much more likely to be working full time while they attended college and thus did not need to rely upon summer jobs. Part-time students were more likely than full-time students to have relied on a spouse's income—probably more women relied on their husband's incomes than vice versa because more women than men enrolled part time. Full-time adult students might have been younger than the part-timers; if so, these differences in aid patterns seem reasonable.

It is not clear whether the availability of public subsidies to certain adults encourages them to attend full time or, more likely, those who attend full time are eligible for more subsidies. Much of the financial burden on adults results from institutions charging higher rates per credit hour or minimum fees per semester (that is, half of the full-time credit load) for part-time students (Westervelt 1975). Fixed costs per registrant may be a justifiable reason that higher per-course costs are imposed upon part-time students. However, "if adults are expected to pay fuller educational costs than their younger counterparts, their access to degree opportunities (if it is a degree they are pursuing) is likely to remain a secondary priority of the institutions that host baccalaureate programs for adults" (Eldred and Marienau 1979, p. 39).

Adult students followed distinct patterns of financing their educations by employment status: There were part-time students who worked full time and full-time students who either received support from family or summer jobs or who competed with traditional students for the usual sources of aid.

To what extent greater accessibility of public aid would encourage more adults to attend full time is unclear. Surely, for many, education must come second to a full-time job.

Source of first year's educational expenses was also examined by marital status for the years 1975 and 1978 (see table A-9). The category of work and savings was especially important for unmarried adult students. For those who were married and living with spouses, the main source of financing the first year of college was their spouses. GI benefits from their military service was an important source for many adult students in this category in 1975, but more so for men than women (see tables A-10 and A-11). The BEOG was an important source of financing education for adult students, especially for women who were married but not living with their spouses.

The financial aid situations of the adult students must be looked at very differently from those of their traditional-age counterparts. Traditional-age students usually were supported by their parental families. Financial need for them is determined by parental family income. Adult students generally relied on their own or their spouse's incomes or savings to finance their educations. Married adult students, especially those with families, have financial responsiblities that younger, unmarried students do not have. For example, a married woman with a husband earning a relatively high income still might place a tremendous financial burden on her family by returning to school (for example, the cost of child care), yet most financial aid programs have had limits on family earnings for eligibility. A traditional-age student can declare herself independent of parents but a married female adult student with children cannot declare herself independent of her spouse. So the financial situation of the younger student from an upper-income family cannot be compared with that of the married adult student from the same "family" income level.

When the source of financing the first year's educational expenses was examined by father's educational attainment, it became apparent that off-spring from different educational backgrounds financed their educations differently (see table A-12). Although work and savings were important for adults regardless of father's educational attainment, gifts or parental or family aid were significantly relied upon by adults whose parents had obtained college degrees or postgraduate degrees. The BEOG was relied upon more by adults whose parents had less education than by those whose parents had more education. Also, GI benefits from their military service were used more in 1974 by adults whose parents had less than a college education than by those whose parents had more than a college education. Probably people from low-SES backgrounds were more likely to enter the military.

Despite the slightly greater concerns expressed by adults regarding their ability to finance a college education, adult access to resources did not seem to be much worse than the access of younger students for those in our samples. This implies that the expenses of adults are greater than those of traditional-age students and that financial aid (regardless of amount) covers fewer of their costs of living. In the future, opportunities to obtain GI benefits may no longer be available to as many people as they were in the past. But the elimination of limits on earnings for loan eligibility may compensate for this loss, particularly because adults are more receptive to loans than younger students are.

As eligibility limits on other federal programs, particularly BEOG, are raised, these programs should become more accessible to adults. And most adults have higher earnings and more savings than traditional students. In the future, traditional students may not be able to rely on parental help to finance their college educations as much as they did in the past because of the effect of inflation on savings.

What has not been considered in this analysis is the actual *amount* of aid given to adult and younger students. But dollar amounts are probably not much higher for adults, given their overrepresentation in low-cost institutions. That is, considering the greater expenses of adults with families, the main problem with current financing methods may be that they channel adults into two-year colleges. The challenge for other kinds of colleges and universities will be to devise financing programs that will enable adults to look beyond the public two-year colleges when making their choices. In view of the recent research on the impact of college (Astin 1977), it is possible that if adults can attend four-year colleges, universities, and higher quality institutions in general, the benefits to the adult students and to society may be greatly increased. This assumes that what is most beneficial for traditional students (only part-time work, full-time attendance, four-year rather than two-year colleges, residential living) will also be most beneficial for adults. In reality, adult students probably do not need these conditions in order to get the most from college. They are more mature, their motivation is evident from the sacrifices they make to attend, and adults are more likely to look beyond the campus for social and leisure activities.

5 Preparation for College

More adults than traditional-age students in our sample indicated that they were poorly prepared for college. However, some scholars question whether adults are actually less prepared than their younger counterparts or just less confident of their capabilities. Some suggest that adults just think that they are less prepared, which deters many of them from entering college at all. Results from our data indicate however that adults' beliefs in this area are probably accurate. The results strongly support the view that adults will need special help if they are to benefit from college as much as others do.

From 1974 to 1978 many more adults than traditional-age students (33.3 percent compared with 15 percent) said they were not in a college-preparatory program in high school (see table 5-1). The data indicate that black adults were substantially less likely than white adults or other minority-group members to have been in college-preparatory high-school programs (55 percent of blacks, 67 percent of whites, and 63 percent of other races had been in college-preparatory programs in 1974; in 1978 the numbers were 58, 69, and 68 percent respectively). The higher the parental income, the more likely adult students were to have been in college-preparatory programs: In 1974, 56 percent of adults from families with incomes below $4,000 were in college-preparatory programs and this proportion rose to 81 percent of the adults from families with incomes over $30,000. In 1978 the participation in college-preparatory programs ranged from 59 percent of adults with family incomes of less than $4,000 to 83 percent of adults with family incomes of $30,000 or more. This finding holds for members of each race separately as well. Similar patterns were revealed when father's education was considered: The more educated one's father, the more likely an adult student was to have been in a college-preparatory program. Also, as would be expected, those with higher grades were more likely to have been preparing for college while in high school.

Most adults in postsecondary education came from families with incomes of $10,000 or more (Indiana Commission of Higher Education 1979). If low-SES adults return to college to make up for earlier educational deprivation, they come less well prepared than high-SES returning adults and contemporary traditional-age students. The nature of the student population will change as more low-SES adults enter college, and remediation needs will have to be determined.

Table 5-1

Type of High-School Program, for all Institutions, by Year and Student Type (Traditional and Adult)

(in percentages)

	1974		1975		1976		1977		1978	
	T	A	T	A	T	A	T	A	T	A
College-preparatory	87	64	86	64	86	66	86	66	88	67
Other	13	36	14	36	14	34	14	34	12	33

T = CIRP norms participants, A = adult participants.
Data unavailable for the years prior to 1974.

Part-timers who started college in both 1974 and 1978 were less likely to have participated in college-preparatory programs than their full-time peers. Fifty-seven percent of the part-time adults in 1974 and 62 percent in 1978 had been in college-preparatory courses. The corresponding figures for full-time adult students were 66 and 68 percent respectively. However differences declined over time. Because the CIRP adult sample overrepresents full-time adult students, it also overstates the extent to which adults in college had been in high-school college-preparatory programs. However, differences are not great enough to cause us to revise our overall conclusions.

Curriculum Preparation in High School

The question regarding curriculum preparation—available from 1975 to 1978—was examined to determine how much preparation was offered in high school (see table 5-2). Respondents' reports indicated that high schools

Table 5-2

"Poor Curriculum Preparation at My High School," for Adult Respondents, for all Institutions by Year

(in percentages)

	1975	1976	1977	1978
Mathematical skills	26	27	26	26
Reading and composition	15	16	14	14
Foreign language	54	51	50	47
Science	18	18	18	18
History, social sciences	10	11	10	10
Vocational skills	39	40	40	38
Musical and artistic skills	43	43	41	41
Study habits	29	30	29	31

Data unavailable for the years prior to 1975.

prepared adult students least effectively in foreign languages, music, art, and vocational skills, and prepared them most effectively in history and social sciences, reading and composition, and scientific subjects. Differences in preparation of part- and full-time adult students were slight. Full-timers had more preparation in mathematics, foreign languages, and science but less preparation in vocational skills.

In 1978 adults had had much poorer preparation in all academic areas and in study habits than younger students had. However vocational and artistic preparation was about equal. This was true when comparisons were made between adult and younger students at different kinds of institutions as well.

Remedial Help

A question regarding need for remediation was available in 1971 and 1972 and from 1976 to 1978 (see table 5-3). Mathematics was the subject in which most of the adult and traditional-age students needed remedial help; social studies was the subject in which both groups of students were least in need of remedial help. Generally, adults felt more in need of remediation than traditional-age students did in all subjects, especially in the most recent years. In 1978 there were few differences between part- and full-time adult students in their perceptions of needing remedial help. These data correspond to our previous findings regarding attendance in college-preparatory programs. Adults may feel they need more tutoring than younger students because they have been away from formal education.

Nevertheless, with one exception, there is a perfect rank-order correlation between subjects for which adults were poorly prepared and subjects in which they needed tutoring. The exception is that mathematics was the primary subject in which tutoring was required whereas students' preparation was poorest in foreign languages. Mathematical techniques have changed a great deal since the adult respondents were in high school. Also, research suggests that adults perform less well on those tasks that they do not use (for example, grammar and math) and better on those that they do use (for example, social studies and literature). But math is a basic tool for all curricular areas. This finding raises major questions regarding differences in performance on entrance exams and possible age discrimination in requirements.

As we noted earlier, measures of the degree of preparation and the need for remediation are subjective rather than objective evaluations by the students. Differences between adult and traditional-age students may reflect differences in self-confidence rather than true differences in preparation. For example, adults may feel poorly prepared for the academic routine

Table 5-3
"Perceived Need of Tutoring," for All Institutions, by Year and Student Type (Traditional and Adult)
(in percentages)

Need Tutoring in:	1971		1972		1976		1977		1978	
	T	*A*	*T*	*A*	*T*	*A*	*T*	*A*	*T*	*A*
English	16	22	20	27	—	20	13	21	14	21
Reading	11	11	11	13	—	11	7	11	8	13
Mathematics	36	39	39	44	—	33	26	36	25	36
Social Studies	4	4	5	6	—	4	2	5	4	10
Science	21	15	22	18	—	12	10	14	13	20
Foreign language	21	20	22	22	—	13	12	17	14	23

T = CIRP norms participants, A = adult participants.
Data unavailable for the following years: 1966, 1967, 1968, 1969, 1970, 1973, 1974, 1975.

because they have been out of school for a long time. Perhaps refresher courses would help prepare them better than remedial work for the return to college. The perceptions of adults however may explain why more adults do not enroll: They feel they are not qualified to attend college.

High-School Grade-Point Average

If adults achieved lower grades in high school than their younger colleagues, it might be reasonable to infer that adults were less prepared for college.

Generally, the younger students came to college with higher grade-point averages than their adult counterparts (more A and B averages) (see table 5-4). The adult students had more B and C averages upon entering college. However a B average was the most common for both traditional and adult students. More adult students than younger students had D averages. Grade-point averages, in general, increased as the years progressed. A common explanation for this is grade inflation.

Returning adults may have decided not to go directly from high school to college because of their low grades, in which case the inferior preparation is emphasized. However, the grade inflation phenomenon is widely known these days—what once was C work is considered B work today. So grade differences between adult and traditional students may not reflect real differences in high-school achievement. On the other hand, the data presented earlier about the need for remedial help indicate that differences may indeed exist.

Table 5-5 confirms the obvious—that most adults from 1973 to 1978 delayed entry into college for some time while the younger, traditional-age students went directly from high school to college. Although far from the

Table 5-4
High-School Grade-Point Average, for All Institutions, by Year and Student Type (Traditional and Adult)
(in percentages)

	High School GPA			
	A	B	C	D
1966				
Traditional	16	54	30	1
Adult	7	42	48	3
1967				
Traditional	14	55	30	1
Adult	7	45	46	3
1968				
Traditional	14	55	31	1
Adult	6	44	47	3
1969				
Traditional	12	56	32	1
Adult	6	42	49	3
1970				
Traditional	14	57	27	1
Adult	4	46	47	3
1971				
Traditional	15	58	25	1
Adult	7	44	46	3
1972				
Traditional	18	59	23	1
Adult	7	46	44	2
1973				
Traditional	18	63	21	0
Adult	6	49	42	2
1974				
Traditional	19	60	22	0
Adult	7	45	45	2
1975				
Traditional	18	61	21	0
Adult	7	48	43	2
1976				
Traditional	19	61	20	0
Adult	8	48	42	3
1977				
Traditional	20	62	18	0
Adult	9	50	39	2
1978				
Traditional	23	59	17	0
Adult	10	51	36	2

Table 5-5
Year Adult and Traditional-Age Respondents Graduated from High School, for All Institutions, by Year
(in percentages)

	1973		1974		1975		1976		1977		1978	
	T	A	T	A	T	A	T	A	T	A	T	A
Same year as entered	93	1	92	1	92	1	93	1	93	1	94	1
Earlier than freshman year	6	86	6	84	6	84	6	86	6	86	5	88
High school equivalency (GED)	1	11	1	11	1	13	1	12	1	10	—	10
Never completed high school	1	2	1	4	1	3	—	3	—	2	—	2

T = CIRP norms participants, A = adult participants.
Data unavailable for the years prior to 1973.

majority, a significant number of adults never graduated from high school but took the high-school-equivalency test (GED) before entering college. Nevertheless at least 84 percent of the adult students in the CIRP sample in each year between 1973 and 1978 had graduated from high school. And between 10 and 13 percent had entered college after taking a high-school-equivalency test. If we can generalize from these data, only one out of eight adults in college entered via the GED route. And about 4 percent never even achieved high-school equivalency; these adults probably attended two-year colleges.

A final aspect of their preparation for college is the extent to which adult students had previously taken college-level courses. Tables 5-6 and 5-7 compare the previous college course experiences of part-time and full-time adult students in 1974 and 1978. Full-timers were more likely than part-timers to have taken courses for credit at community colleges (27 percent versus 18 percent in 1974, and 31 percent versus 22 percent in 1978) and at four-year colleges or universities other than the one presently attended (24 percent versus 20 percent in 1974, and 27 percent versus 22 percent in 1978). About 5 percent of each group had taken noncredit courses. Slightly more part-timers had taken either credit or noncredit courses at technical or vocational schools. However part-time adults were more likely to have taken courses for credit previously at their current institutions, probably because of their greater commitments to particular localities.

Table 5-6
Courses Taken by Adult Respondents at Any Other Institution, by Enrollment Status and Year
(in percentages)

	1974		1978	
	Part-time	Full-time	Part-time	Full-time
No credit at any other institution	21	20	19	17
No noncredit at any other institution	24	22	22	21
Credit at a junior or community college	18	27	22	31
Noncredit at a junior or community college	4	4	5	5
Credit at a four-year college or university	20	24	22	27
Noncredit at a four-year college or university	4	3	5	4
Credit at some other postsecondary school (technical, vocational, or business)	14	11	17	14
Noncredit at some other postsecondary school (technical, vocational, or business)	18	14	18	14

Table 5-7
Courses Taken for Credit by Adult Respondents at this Institution, by Enrollment Status and Year
(in percentages)

	1974		1978	
	Part-time	*Full-time*	*Part-time*	*Full-time*
No	74	78	73	81
Yes	26	22	27	19

Thus approximately one-quarter of the adults had taken college courses previously, which gave them some advantages in facing their new college experiences.

6 College Plans

Living Arrangements

Although only one-quarter of the adult students indicated that their college choice was significantly influenced by their desire to live at home, this factor was twice as important to them as it was to younger students (see table 3-3). Moreover, roughly 80 percent of the adult students lived within commuting distance of their colleges (fifty miles or less), compared with about half of the traditional students. In every year, between 35 and 50 percent of the adults lived less than ten miles from their colleges, compared with less than 30 percent of the younger students who lived this close. It seems that an eleven- to fifty-mile distance became more of an option for adult students as the years progressed. These trends are probably due to differences in marital status and family situation; that is, adults were more likely to be married and to have had children.

Those coming from families where the father graduated from college or obtained a postgraduate degree tended to travel greater distances to school. In 1973 they either stayed within ten miles of their home or traveled more than five hundred miles away.

Again, younger students usually have fewer family and job-related responsibilities than older students so they are usually more mobile. Over one-third of the younger students lived more than one hundred miles away from their colleges, whereas only one-quarter of the adults did. However, the adults were more likely to move away from home in later years. The fact that adults are beginning to travel greater distances to school may be due to the relative ease with which people commute, or perhaps to the fact that attitudes toward marriage and family responsibilities no longer restrict the mobility of adult students as much as they used to.

Table 6-1 indicates that a higher proportion of adult women than adult men attended college within one hundred miles of home. However the differences were infrequently greater than ten percentage points. The hypothesis that led to the development of this table was that women might be significantly less mobile than men with regard to college choice (Westervelt 1975). Although women revealed a slight tendency to stay nearer to home, the data did not reveal major differences in mobility. At least three-quarters of both male and female adult freshmen remained within one hundred miles of home.

Table 6-1
Distance from Home to College of Adult Respondents, by Year and Sex
(in percentages)

	100 Miles or Less	*Over 100 Miles*
1969		
Males	82	18
Females	90	10
1970		
Males	82	18
Females	86	14
1971		
Males	81	19
Females	90	10
1972		
Males	69	31
Females	78	22
1973		
Males	70	30
Females	77	23
1975		
Males	70	30
Females	78	22
1976		
Males	67	33
Females	77	23
1977		
Males	67	33/
Females	77	23
1978		
Males	79	21
Females	90	10

Data unavailable for the following years: 1966, 1967, 1968, 1974.

Approximately half of the traditional-age students planned to live in college dormitories rather than in fraternities, sororities, or other kinds of student housing. Most adults planned to live in private homes or apartments that were probably nonparental (about 50 percent) or in other noncampus facilities (21 percent in 1973 and 14 percent in 1978). These data appear in table 6-2. Adults do not take advantage of subsidized student housing, which probably contributes significantly to their greater expenses. Adults may simply not be interested in participating in the social activity on campus. Or the lack of on-campus housing for adults, especially married adults, may deter many from returning to college.

Another option adult respondents had in this choice set was living with parents or relatives. One-quarter of the adults had plans of this kind, but probably most of them were living with spouses rather than parents. Be-

Table 6-2
Miles from Home and Where Plan to Live Next Fall, for All Institutions, by Year and Student Type (Traditional and Adult)
(in percentages)

	1969		1970		1971		1972		1973		1974		1975		1976		1977		1978	
	T	A	T	A	T	A	T	A	T	A	T	A	T	A	T	A	T	A	T	A
Miles from home																				
10 or less	6	54	27	54	23	53	27	40	28	41	—	—	26	40	29	36	27	35	22	49
11-50	24	24	25	25	27	26	25	26	25	25	—	—	26	27	26	29	26	29	26	31
51-100	13	6	13	4	15	6	14	7	13	6	—	—	13	7	13	7	14	7	15	5
101-500	26	9	27	13	28	9	26	12	26	13	—	—	26	11	24	11	25	10	28	7
More than 500	9	7	9	4	8	6	9	16	8	15	—	—	8	15	8	17	7	17	8	7
Where plan to live next fall																				
Parents or relatives	—		—		—		—		42	22	22	23	39	23	44	24	22	24	19	24
Other private home, apartment, or room	—		—		—		—		5	47	28	52	7	49	7	50	26	50	25	48
College dormitory	—		—		—		—		50	8	40	7	51	8	47	9	42	10	46	12
Fraternity or sorority house	—		—		—		—		0	0	4	0	0	0	0	0	4	0	4	0
Other campus student housing	—		—		—		—		1	2	3	1	2	2	1	2	4	2	4	2
Other	—		—		—		—		1	21	3	16	1	19	1	14	2	15	2	14

T = CIRP norms participants.
A = Adult Participants.
Data unavailable for the years prior to 1969.

tween 20 and 40 percent of the younger students indicated this arrangement, but they were more likely to be living with parents and to be subsidized.

As table 6-3 indicates, virtually no part-time adult students lived in college dormitories, fraternities, or sororities, or other campus housing. Approximately equal numbers of full- and part-time adult students lived with parents or relatives and in other private homes, apartments, or rooms. The fact that part-time adult students selected the option "other" indicates that they probably lived with a spouse, in a family situation. Again, differences by enrollment status were not great.

Astin (1977) found that the most important environmental characteristic associated with remaining in college was living in a dormitory during the freshman year. According to Astin, residential living fosters involvement with the college or university, which in turn leads to greater persistence rates and more positive impacts for traditional students. However, it has not been shown that these relationships hold for adult students as well. Although residential living is important in motivating young college students, adults who attend are probably sufficiently motivated to attend and persist without the involvement that comes from living on campus with other students. Those who enter college immediately after high school may do so because this is expected of them or because no better options seem available. Thus some postenrollment stimuli are needed to motivate them. On the other hand, adults who enter or return to college have made an explicit decision that probably involves significant sacrifices of income, family life, recreation, and so on.

Degree Aspirations

For most of the adult and traditional-age students, the highest academic degrees aspired to over the thirteen-year period were the bachelor's degree and the master's degree (see table 6-4). Although it appears that adults had lower aspirations than younger students (more traditional students aspired to professional degrees), perhaps the adults' aspirations are just more specific than those of younger students. These findings are consistent with the human capital theory, in that adults will have a shorter period of time over which to enjoy the benefits (financial and other) of college attendance. Thus, the incentives for them to incur the cost of advanced, postcollege education are lower than they would be for younger students. The degree aspirations of adults increased over time so that by 1978, 43 percent of adults planned to obtain either a master's degree (31 percent) or a doctorate (12 percent). This was true regardless of institutional type. As table 6-5 shows, adults in four-year and predominantly black colleges had higher degree aspirations than those in two-year colleges and slightly higher aspira-

Table 6-3
**Living Arrangements of Adult Respondents, by Enrollment Status
and Year**
(in percentages)

Living Arrangements	1974		1978	
	Part-time	*Full-time*	*Part-time*	*Full-time*
With parents or relatives	24	23	25	23
Other private home, apartment, or room	50	53	52	48
College dormitory	0	9	1	15
Fraternity or sorority house	0	0	0	0
Other campus student housing	0	2	0	2
Other	25	13	22	12

tions than adults in universities, at least where the master's degree was concerned. If it will benefit society to have adults acquire advanced degrees, policies are needed to encourage or enable adults to attend four-year rather than two-year institutions. (It could be that those with lower degree aspirations choose two-year colleges. But the two-year college experience probably does not elevate these goals.) It makes sense that the aspirations of adults have increased because the higher level of educational attainment in the general society allows employers to "raise the screen." Today an associate's degree is often required for entry level positions that once required a high-school diploma. As table 6-6 indicates, part-time adults in 1974 and 1978 were more likely than full-timers to seek no degree at all, or to seek an associate's degree or a bachelor's degree. Full-time adults were more likely to seek advanced graduate or professional degrees. Again, the overrepresentation of full-time students in the CIRP adult sample probably overstates the adult students' degree aspirations.

In 1978 students who were unmarried and those who were married but not living with their spouses had higher aspirations than those who were married and living with their spouses (see table 6-7). When marital status by highest degree planned was broken down by sex, women, regardless of marital status, had lower degree aspirations than men. Ability to finance advanced education is reflected in this finding.

Probable Major

This question was presented in all thirteen years that the CIRP questionnaires were administered. Business was the most popular major for adult students, but selection of a probable major differed by institutional type

Table 6-4
Highest Degree Planned Anywhere, for All Institutions, by Year and Student Type (Traditional and Adult)
(in percentages)

Highest Degree Planned	1966 T	1966 A	1967 T	1967 A	1968 T	1968 A	1969 T	1969 A	1970 T	1970 A	1972 T	1972 A	1973 T	1973 A	1974 T	1974 A	1975 T	1975 A	1976 T	1976 A	1977 T	1977 A	1978 T	1978 A
None	6	6	4	5	4	4	2	2	2	3	3	4	4	4	4	6	4	4	3	4	2	4	2	3
Associate (A.A. or equivalent)	6	9	7	10	7	10	9	11	8	17	8	12	6	8	8	12	8	13	8	10	8	10	8	10
Bachelor's (B.A., B.S.)	39	42	37	41	38	38	38	37	38	38	37	35	31	31	27	34	35	33	36	34	36	31	37	34
Master's (M.A., M.S.)	32	28	32	30	32	31	33	32	31	26	27	27	32	33	27	27	28	27	29	29	30	31	30	31
Ph.D. or Ed.D.	10	9	10	9	11	10	10	11	10	7	9	10	11	13	8	10	9	11	9	11	9	12	9	12
M.D., D.O., D.D.S., or D.V.M.	5	2	5	2	4	2	4	3	5	2	7	4	8	4	8	4	7	4	7	4	6	4	7	4
LL.B. or J.D. (law)	2	1	1	1	1	1	2	2	4	2	4	3	3	3	4	3	5	3	5	3	5	4	4	3
B.D. or M. Div. (divinity)	0	0	0	0	0	0	0	0	0	1	0	1	0	1	0	1	1	1	1	1	0	1	0	1
Other	2	2	2	2	2	2	2	2	3	4	3	3	2	3	3	3	4	5	3	4	3	4	2	3

T = CIRP norms participants, A = adult participants.
Data unavailable for 1971.

Table 6-5
Highest Degree Planned for Adult Respondents, by Type of Institution and Year
(in percentages)

Highest Degree Planned	1974				1978			
	All Two-year Colleges	All Four-year Colleges	All Universities	Predominantly Black Colleges	All Two-year Colleges	All Four-year Colleges	All Universities	Predominantly Black Colleges
None	10	2	2	4	6	2	1	3
Associate (A.A. or equivalent)	19	5	6	9	21	4	3	5
Bachelor's (B.A., B.S.)	37	31	33	30	38	34	31	25
Master's (M.A., M.S.)	21	36	29	35	21	36	34	36
Ph.D. or Ed.D	6	13	15	14	5	13	18	21
M.D., D.O., D.D.S., or D.V.M.	2	5	6	4	2	4	7	4
LL.B. or J.D. (law)	2	3	6	2	1	3	5	3
B.D. or M.Div. (divinity)	1	2	1	0	1	2	0	1
Other	4	2	2	2	5	3	1	2

Table 6-6
Highest Degree Planned for Adult Respondents, by Enrollment Status and Year
(in percentages)

	1974		1978	
	Part-time	Full-time	Part-time	Full-time
None	12	4	5	3
Associate (A.A. or equivalent)	17	11	14	8
Bachelor's degree (B.A., B.S.)	40	32	44	31
Master's degree (M.A., M.S.)	19	29	25	32
Ph.D. or Ed.D.	4	12	6	14
M.D., D.O., D.D.S., D.V.M.	1	4	1	5
LL.B. or J.D. (law)	1	3	2	3
B.D. or M.Div. (divinity)	0	1	0	1
Other	4	3	3	3

(see tables 6-8 and 6-9). For example, in 1978 business was much more popular for adult students at two-year and predominantly black colleges than at four-year colleges and all universities. Engineering, which was popular as a major in the first five years that this question was available, became much less popular in the 1970s. Health professions, education, and the social sciences were relatively frequent choices as probable majors of adult freshmen.

The humanities and liberal arts departments were not popular with either traditional-age students or adults. Unfortunately these are the very departments that need adults most to fill seats. Some adults may have enrolled in humanities subjects because of requirements in their majors, but it is extremely difficult to determine whether they are electing to study these subjects. Adults seem to attend college for reasons of convenience—if a business major is available, they will attend a nearby college and fulfill humanities requirements if necessary. Perhaps colleges with liberal arts programs will make changes to accommodate adult learners. Glover (1979) contends that small liberal arts colleges facing declining enrollments will shift to more career-oriented programs.

Business and education were popular probable majors for traditional-age students, while their choice of engineering followed a pattern over the years similar to that of their adult counterparts.

The categories of least frequently chosen majors for both adult and traditional-age students were: agriculture, biological sciences, humanities, mathematics and statistics, physical sciences, and "undecided." However traditional-age students considered these majors to be slightly more desirable than adult students did. Perhaps this is because adults enroll in

Table 6-7
Marital Status of Adult Respondents, by Highest Degree Planned and Year
(in percentages)

Highest Degree Planned	1975			1978		
	Unmarried	*Married, Living with Spouse*	*Married, Not Living with Spouse*	*Unmarried*	*Married, Living with Spouse*	*Married, Not Living with Spouse*
None	4	4	5	3	3	4
Associate (A.A. or equivalent)	9	16	15	7	13	12
Bachelor's degree (B.A., B.S.)	31	36	30	32	38	30
Master's degree (M.A., M.S.)	29	25	28	32	29	30
Ph.D. or Ed.D	12	9	10	14	8	14
M.D., D.O., D.D.S., D.V.M.	5	3	3	5	3	4
LL.B. or J.D. (law)	3	2	3	3	2	3
B.D. or M.Div. (divinity)	1	2	1	1	1	1
Other	5	4	6	3	3	3

Table 6-8
Probable Major, for All Institutions, by Year and Student Type (Traditional and Adult)
(in percentages)

Probable Major	1966 T	1966 A	1967 T	1967 A	1968 T	1968 A	1969 T	1969 A	1970 T	1970 A	1971 T	1971 A	1972 T	1972 A	1973 T	1973 A	1974 T	1974 A	1975 T	1975 A	1976 T	1976 A	1977 T	1977 A	1978 T	1978 A
Agriculture	2	3	2	2	2	2	2	2	2	2	3	2	3	2	3	2	4	2	4	2	4	2	4	2	3	1
Biological sciences	4	2	4	2	4	2	3	2	4	2	4	3	4	2	7	4	7	4	6	4	6	4	5	4	5	3
Business	14	19	16	21	16	22	16	22	16	23	16	19	18	18	18	18	18	18	19	18	21	19	22	19	24	20
Education	11	9	10	9	12	9	11	9	12	7	10	7	7	5	12	9	10	8	10	8	9	8	9	9	8	8
Engineering[a]	10	6	10	16	10	12	10	12	9	11	7	7	7	7	7	7	7	6	8	6	8	7	9	7	10	7
English	4	3	4	3	4	3	4	3	3	2	2	2	2	2	2	2	2	2	2	1	2	1	2	1	2	2
Health professional	5	7	5	8	5	10	6	9	7	14	9	14	11	17	10	16	4	15	4	15	3	15	7	14	6	16
History and political sciences[b]	7	4	7	5	7	5	6	5	5	4	4	4	4	3	—	3	2	3	2	2	2	3	3	2	3	2
Humanities	5	3	5	3	4	4	4	3	4	4	3	4	4	4	3	4	7	4	6	4	6	4	2	3	1	3
Fine arts[a]	8	7	9	6	9	7	9	7	9	7	9	8	9	7	7	6	8	7	7	6	7	6	6	7	6	6
Mathematics and statistics	4	2	4	2	4	2	4	2	3	1	3	1	2	1	2	1	1	1	1	1	1	1	1	1	1	1
Physical sciences	3	3	3	2	3	2	2	2	2	1	2	2	2	1	3	2	3	2	3	2	3	2	2	2	2	2
Preprofessional[c]	7	4	7	4	6	4	6	4	7	4	8	6	9	6	—	—	—	—	—	—	—	—	3	3	3	2
Social sciences[b]	8	8	8	8	8	9	9	10	9	9	9	11	8	10	—	11	7	11	6	10	6	9	5	9	5	9
Other fields (technical)[a]	2	4	3	5	3	5	4	5	4	6	5	7	6	9	5	7	8	9	9	10	8	8	8	8	8	8
Other fields (nontechnical)[a]	3	2	2	2	2	2	2	2	2	1	3	2	3	2	7	7	10	9	10	9	11	9	8	8	9	8
Undecided	2	1	2	1	2	1	2	1	2	1	2	1	2	2	2	2	2	2	2	2	2	2	3	3	5	2

T = CIRP norms participants, A = adult participants.

[a] From 1966 to 1972 and 1977 to 1978, the category of fine arts included architecture and the category of other fields (technical) included other professional. From 1973 to 1976, fine arts was included in the engineering category and other professional was included in other fields (nontechnical). These four majors are therefore not directly comparable across all of the years.

[b] Percentages for history and political science and social science are not presented in 1973 for traditional-age respondents because they were calculated differently in the published norms reports.

[c] The category of preprofessional major wsa not available from 1973 to 1976.

Table 6-9
Probable Major for 1978 Adult Respondents, by Type of Institution
(in percentages)

	All Two-year Colleges	All Four-year Colleges	All Universities	Predominantly Black Colleges
Agriculture	2	1	1	2
Biological sciences	2	3	6	4
Business	24	19	15	25
Education	6	11	6	10
Engineering	6	7	8	8
English	1	2	2	1
Health professional	22	14	13	11
History and political science	1	2	3	3
Humanities	2	4	4	1
Fine arts	4	7	8	6
Mathematics and statistics	0	0	0	1
Physical sciences	1	1	3	1
Preprofessional	1	2	3	1
Social science	5	11	12	9
Other fields (technical)	12	5	5	9
Other fields (nontechnical)	8	8	6	8
Undecided	2	2	2	1

college with specific goals, whereas traditional-age students often experiment with subjects that sound interesting but are not practical or worthy of four years of study.

Table 6-10 indicates substantial similarities in probable major between part-time and full-time students. The only difference between the two groups was that many more of the part-time than full-time adults planned to major in business. The CIRP sample probably understated adult interest in business programs. This is an important finding given the hope expressed by humanities programs (and others that are suffering excessive enrollment declines) that returning adults will fill the empty seats in their classrooms.

Choice of probable major did not differ for adults by marital status (see table A-13) but men were more interested in business majors while women were more interested in the health professions.

Institutional Quality

Adults chose and enrolled in institutions with lower admissions standards than their traditional-age counterparts, but the institutions' reputation as a whole may be irrelevant in most adults' decision making. The adult student may consider instead the quality of particular departments or programs within an institution. For instance, he or she may choose to attend a

Table 6-10
Probable Major of Adult Respondents, by Enrollment Status and Year
(in percentages)

	1974		1978	
	Part-time	*Full-time*	*Part-time*	*Full-time*
Agriculture	1	2	1	2
Biological sciences	2	5	2	4
Business	25	15	28	18
Education	7	8	7	8
Engineering[a]	5	6	5	8
English	2	2	2	2
Health professional	16	14	15	16
History and political science	1	3	1	2
Humanities	3	4	3	3
Fine arts[a]	6	7	5	6
Mathematics and statistics	0	1	1	0
Physical sciences	1	2	1	2
Preprofessional[b]	—	—	0	2
Social science	9	11	9	9
Other fields (technical)[a]	9	10	8	8
Other fields (nontechnical)[a]	9	9	8	8
Undecided	3	2	4	2

[a]In 1978 the category of fine arts included architecture and the category of other fields (technical) included other professional. In 1974 fine arts was included in the engineering category and other professional was included in other fields (nontechnical). These four majors are therefore not directly comparable across the two years.
[b]The category of preprofessional major was not available in 1974.

relatively nonselective institution because of particular interests; the health science or business departments, for example, may be of high quality. Or the more selective institutions may not have as many departments as less selective institutions do.

Probable Career Occupation

After the nonspecified "other" category, the career occupation most often selected by adult freshmen over the years was businessman (see table 6-11). Between 1966 and 1970, secondary educator and engineer were popular, and nurse was popular from 1970 on. As would be expected, businessman and engineer were popular choices for adult men, and nurse was a popular choice for adult women.

There were few differences between adult students and traditional-age students in anticipating an occupation. However, adult students were more confident of their probable career occupations, whereas a significant number of traditional-age students were undecided about probable career

Table 6-11
Probable Career Occupation, for All Institutions, by Year and Student Type (Traditional and Adult)
(in percentages)

	1966		1967		1968		1969		1970		1971		1972		1973		1974		1975		1976		1977		1978	
	T	A	T	A	T	A	T	A	T	A	T	A	T	A	T	A	T	A	T	A	T	A	T	A	T	A
Artist (including performer)	7	5	8	4	6	4	6	4	6	4	6	6	6	6	—	5	6	6	5	4	7	7	7	7	6	7
Businessman	12	18	3	18	11	18	11	18	11	18	11	15	10	10	16	16	13	14	14	14	16	16	18	16	19	17
Clergyman	1	1	0	2	1	2	1	2	1	2	1	2	1	1	1	2	1	2	1	2	2	2	0	2	0	2
College teacher	5	2	2	2	4	2	3	2	4	2	1	3	6	3	2	2	5	2	5	2	5	3	4	4	4	3
Doctor (M.D. or D.D.S.)	2	3	2	2	2	2	2	2	1	1	4	3	1	2	6	3	1	2	1	2	0	1	0	1	0	1
Educator (secondary)	14	10	19	10	14	11	13	10	11	6	9	5	6	5	—	4	4	3	4	3	4	4	3	3	3	3
Elementary teacher	8	7	18	8	9	7	9	7	8	6	7	5	6	5	4	3	5	4	6	3	8	6	8	4	9	7
Engineer	9	15	0	13	8	10	8	10	8	9	5	6	6	5	—	5	5	4	6	4	8	6	8	7	9	7
Farmer or forester	2	3	1	2	2	2	2	2	2	2	3	2	3	2	3	2	4	2	4	2	3	2	3	2	2	1
Health professional	5	3	6	3	4	3	4	4	4	3	6	5	7	5	9	8	9	8	9	8	7	6	7	6	6	5
Lawyer	4	2	1	2	3	2	4	2	4	2	4	3	5	3	5	3	4	2	4	2	4	3	4	3	4	2
Nurse	2	5	5	6	3	8	3	7	4	11	4	10	5	12	4	12	5	13	5	14	5	13	4	13	4	15
Research scientist	3	2	2	2	3	2	2	2	3	2	2	2	2	2	—	2	2	1	2	2	2	2	2	2	2	2
Other choice[b]	23	21	22	25	20	21	22	22	22	27	24	25	23	27	28	28	26	31	25	29	23	26	23	26	23	25
Undecided	4	2	10	4	11	5	11	6	12	6	13	7	14	7	6	6	12	7	14	8	10	6	10	7	11	7

T = CIRP norms participants, A = adult participants.
[a]Percentages for many of the probable majors of traditional-age respondents in 1973 were not presented here because they were calculated differently in the published norms reports.
[b]From 1966 to 1972 and 1977 to 1978, the category of other choice included psychology. From 1973 to 1976 psychology was included in the category of health professional. These two occupational categories are therefore not directly comparable across all of the years.

occupations, especially in recent years. This was probably because more adults were already working.

Table 6-12 presents data consistent with the statistics on the choice of a major. The largest difference between part-time and full-time adult students' career choices was the part-timers' interest in business management. Careers requiring advanced graduate study were selected less often by part-timers.

This chapter has stressed the similarities between part-time and full-time adult students. Overall, the biases resulting from overrepresentation of full-time students in the CIRP adult sample appear to be small.

Table 6-12

Probable Career Occupation of Adult Respondents, by Enrollment Status and Year

(in percentages)

	1974		1978	
	Part-time	*Full-time*	*Part-time*	*Full-time*
Artist (including performer)	4	6	6	7
Businessman	17	13	22	16
Clergyman	1	2	1	2
College teacher	1	2	1	1
Doctor (M.D. or D.D.S.)	1	3	1	3
Educator (secondary)	2	3	2	3
Elementary teacher	2	3	4	4
Engineer	3	4	5	7
Farmer or forester	1	2	1	1
Health professional[a]	6	8	5	5
Lawyer	1	3	2	2
Nurse	14	12	15	15
Research scientist	1	2	1	2
Other choice[a]	38	30	27	24
Undecided	7	7	9	6

[a]In 1978 the category of other choice included psychology. In 1974 psychology was included in the category of health professional. These two occupational categories were therefore not directly comparable across the two years.

7 Life Goals

College administrators and faculty members must understand what adult students seek to achieve from their postsecondary educational experiences if they hope to assist them to achieve these goals. As Anderson and Darkenwald (1979) have said, "The most powerful predictor of persistence in adult education is satisfaction with the learning activity in terms of its 'helpfulness' in meeting one's objectives" (pp. 4-5). The first part of this chapter describes the goals of adults in the CIRP freshman data base over its thirteen years and compares them with the goals of traditional-age students. If younger students' needs are being met, and if the goals of adults and younger students are similar, then few changes may be required to meet the needs of the new adult clientele. However if adult goals differ from the goals of younger students, more changes will be necessary. The second part of this chapter clarifies the goal patterns of adults by using multiple regression analysis to determine how adults differ in their desires to achieve various life goals.

Important Objectives for Adult Students

Eleven objectives were presented in most of the thirteen years of the CIRP surveys (see table 7-1). We focus on responses that are "essential" or "very important," as opposed to "somewhat important" or "not important," in reporting our data. The first two are referred to as "important" and the second two as "unimportant" to simplify the discussion.

Of the eleven objectives, two were most important over the years to at least 60 percent of adults: to "be an authority in my field" and to "help others in difficulty."

When offered, three objectives were initially important to adult students, but decreased in importance by 1978: to "keep up with political affairs," to "develop a philosophy of life," and to "raise a family." These objectives declined in importance, dropping suddenly in 1971.

Conversely, to "help others in difficulty" increased in importance to adults through 1978. Apparently, adults began to reorder their priorities in attending college at the turn of the decade.

Table 7-1
Objectives Considered "Essential" or "Very Important," for All Institutions, by Year and Student Type (Traditional and Adult)
(in percentages)

	1966		1967		1968		1969		1970		1971		1972		1973		1974		1975		1976		1977		1978	
	T	A	T	A	T	A	T	A	T	A	T	A	T	A	T	A	T	A	T	A	T	A	T	A	T	A
Artistic objectives																										
Achieve in performing art	11	6	11	6	9	4	11	6	13	7	12	8	12	9	20	19	11	9	12	9	12	10	13	12	13	10
Write original works	14	13	14	10	13	10	14	11	10	14	13	13	14	14	—	—	12	14	12	14	13	15	14	17	13	16
Create artistic works	15	14	16	13	14	12	16	14	16	19	15	16	18	19	—	—	14	17	14	17	14	18	16	20	14	18
Perform or compose music	8	4	8	4	6	6	—	—	—	—	—	—	—	—	—	—	—	—	—	—	—	—	—	—	—	—
Status objectives																										
Be an authority in my field	66	70	68	70	58	63	59	64	67	72	60	62	61	62	62	64	62	62	70	68	70	67	75	71	73	68
Obtain recognition from colleagues	48	42	41	37	37	35	41	39	40	37	37	39	37	39	39	—	39	39	43	41	46	42	48	44	50	44
Have administrative responsibility	29	37	25	33	22	30	24	30	22	26	20	27	24	32	27	33	26	29	37	35	32	34	34	35	36	36
Make a theoretical contribution to science	13	16	12	13	10	11	10	12	10	10	9	11	11	13	—	—	13	16	14	16	14	17	14	17	14	17
Become a community leader	30	26	24	22	21	20	18	18	15	14	13	16	18	18	—	—	16	—	16	—	17	—	—	—	—	—
Social objectives																										
Influence the political structure	—	—	—	—	—	—	16	16	18	18	14	16	18	18	15	19	12	15	14	18	15	17	16	17	15	16
Influence social values	—	—	—	—	—	—	34	33	34	32	28	33	38	38	31	40	27	34	36	38	30	35	31	36	31	35
Help others in difficulty	68	61	62	58	59	56	66	63	65	66	63	63	69	69	64	68	61	65	66	70	63	68	65	70	66	70
Be involved in environmental cleanup	—	—	—	—	—	—	—	—	—	—	43	40	45	45	34	38	26	30	29	32	28	30	29	32	28	28
Participate in community action	—	—	—	—	—	—	—	—	29	25	26	28	29	33	31	36	28	32	30	35	29	32	29	34	30	30
Promote racial understanding	58	59	51	52	52	51	51	52	53	56	43	42	49	48	42	46	37	40	39	42	31	38	40	42	42	37
Keep up with political affairs	13	12	19	9	18	9	—	—	20	11	16	11	16	12	—	—	—	—	—	—	—	—	—	—	—	—
Join the Peace Corps or Vista	—	—	—	—	—	—	—	—	—	—	—	—	—	—	—	—	—	—	—	—	—	—	—	—	—	—
Family objectives																										
Raise a family	—	—	—	—	—	—	71	74	68	75	60	65	68	68	56	62	55	69	57	62	57	59	59	60	62	63
Marry in the next five years	—	—	—	—	—	—	—	—	29	17	30	21	34	30	—	—	—	—	—	—	—	—	—	—	—	—
Business objectives																										
Be very well-off financially	44	42	44	38	41	35	44	39	39	34	40	36	37	37	55	48	46	41	50	42	53	43	58	47	60	47
Be successful in my own business	53	49	46	39	45	39	46	39	44	38	42	38	45	41	42	37	39	35	44	38	45	38	47	40	48	39
Be an expert in finance	20	18	12	15	10	13	17	18	16	16	14	15	16	16	—	—	—	—	—	—	—	—	—	—	—	—
Personal objectives																										
Develop a philosophy of life	—	—	83	81	82	82	82	83	76	78	68	72	71	77	69	77	61	71	64	74	61	71	59	71	56	69
Become an outstanding athlete	21	7	14	5	12	5	—	—	—	—	—	—	—	—	—	—	—	—	—	—	—	—	—	—	—	—
Not be obligated to people	28	34	25	27	24	26	24	28	23	26	21	26	23	29	—	—	—	—	—	—	—	—	—	—	—	—
Have an active social life	—	—	—	—	—	—	54	—	57	50	55	40	59	45	—	—	—	—	—	—	—	—	—	—	—	—
Have friends different from me	—	—	—	—	—	—	—	—	—	—	—	—	—	—	—	—	—	—	—	—	—	—	—	—	—	—

T = CIRP norms participants, A = adult participants.

Important Objectives for Traditional-Age Students

Within the eleven consistently presented objectives, the goals important to traditional-age students were the same as those important to adult students. To "be an authority in my field" and to "help others in difficulty" remained consistently important to traditional-age students, while to "keep up with political affairs," to "develop a philosophy of life," and to "raise a family" declined in importance.

These trends reflect a more pragmatic, less altruistic attitude on the part of traditional-age students, as both political idealism and labor market opportunities declined in the 1970s. However, to "develop a philosophy of life" was generally more important to adults than traditional-age students, perhaps reflecting less vocational (or more consumer-oriented) goals for adults who attend college.

Least Important Objectives for Adult Students

Of the eleven choices available in most of the thirteen years, the least important objectives (those with a response rate of 20 percent or less) for adult students were: to "achieve in a performing art," to "write original works," to "create artistic works," and to "make a theoretical contribution to science." Many adults probably felt it was too late for them to attain such goals. It is doubtful that adults would go back to school to achieve such creative goals anyway—even though the goals might be important to them. That is, there are many noncollege programs in most communities that enable adults to partake of the creative arts.

Other objectives that were important to adult students (when presented), perhaps for the same reasons, were: to "perform or compose music," to "influence the political structure," to "join the Peace Corps or Vista," to "be an expert in finance," and to "become an outstanding athlete." To "become a community leader" was important to adult students in four of the seven years it was presented. To "marry in the next five years" was unimportant in one of the three years that it was available as a choice, probably because more adult than traditional students were married already.

Least Important Objectives for Traditional-Age Students

Except for the goal to "marry in the next five years" unimportant goals of traditional-age students were similar to those of adults. To simplify interpretation, the goals from the CIRP questionnaires can be grouped into the following general categories: artistic, status, social, family, business, and personal.

Artistic Objectives

None of the four types of artistic goals was selected by more than 20 percent of adult or traditional-age students in any year. Although the artistic objectives were selected by slightly more traditional-age respondents than adult respondents in the 1960s, in the 1970s slightly more adults selected to "create artistic works" and to "write original works." Only to "achieve in a performing art" was consistently a more important objective to traditional—age students.

Status Objectives

In 1966 and 1978 the status goals of both traditional-age and adult students remained stable, with fluctuations in intervening years. Of the status objectives, to "be an authority in my field" was important to about 70 percent of the adult students. As noted earlier, the least important status objective for adults was to "make a theoretical contribution to science."

All of the status objectives seemed to decline in importance in the late sixties (1968) and started to rise again in the early seventies. By 1978 most of these status objectives returned to the same level of importance they were at in 1966. Of course, traditional values were questioned on campuses across the country between 1968 and 1970.

To "obtain recognition from colleagues" was the only status objective that was consistently more important for traditional-age students than for adult students. To "be an authority in my field" was less important for the traditional-age students until 1974, when it became just as important or more important to the traditional-age students than to the adult students.

Social Objectives

To "help others in difficulty" was the most important social objective for adult students. Not surprisingly, their least important social objective was to "join the Peace Corps or Vista." To "help others in difficulty" was more important for traditional-age students in the sixties and for adult students in the seventies. Other goals that were consistently more important to traditional-age students than to adult students (when offered as choices) were to "influence social values," to "influence the political structure," and to "join the Peace Corps or Vista."

Family Objectives

Not surprisingly, to "raise a family" was a more important family objective for adult students, and to "marry in the next five years" was more important for traditional-age students.

To "raise a family" has decreased in importance over time, and to "marry in the next five years" has increased in importance over time, reflecting the fact that in American society birthrates have declined and divorce rates have increased.

Business Objectives

To "be successful in my own business" was the most important business objective for adult students in the sixties, and to "be very well-off financially" was most important in the seventies. To "be an expert in finance" was the least important business objective for adult students and traditional-age students (when presented).

However all of the business objectives were more important to traditional-age students than to adult students (except "to be an expert in finance"). Adults probably had already achieved in business or were resigned to study for enjoyment rather than career advancement. The only business objective that increased in importance over time for both groups of students was to "be very well-off financially." This reflects the difference in the U.S. economy in the sixties and seventies. In the 1960's, when the U.S. economy was stronger than it is today, financial well-being was viewed by most college attenders as automatic. In recent years, the depressed economic environment has led those in college to be more aware of the importance of striving for financial success.

Personal Objectives

To "develop a philosophy of life" was the most important personal objective for at least 70 percent of the adult students nearly every year it was offered, and to "become an outstanding athlete" was the least important.

All of the personal objectives were more important to the traditional-age students than to the adult students, except to "develop a philosophy of life" and "not [to] be obligated to people." The personal objectives have declined in importance over time for adult students.

In general, adults who enrolled in colleges and universities had a substantially similar range of objectives as the traditional-age student population. Most of the differences are to be expected, easily attributable to age or to the possibility that some objectives offered are not central to the mission of the higher-education system. However, a remaining question is whether changes in higher-education institutions would attract more adults—adults who might consider the traditional programs to be so heavily oriented toward 18-to-21-year-olds that they do not enroll.

Multivariate Analysis

To determine which adults were most interested in certain broad categories of life goals, we used multiple regression (see table 7-2). Four groups of goals were identified for regression analysis: artistic, status, social, and business goals. Two other groups, personal and family goals, were excluded because the relevant questions were not asked in enough years. Interest in each of the four broad groups of goals for each respondent was calculated as the average value (where 4 = essential, 3 = very important, 2 = somewhat important, 1 = not important) of responses for all the questions falling in that category. That is, artistic goals included the desire to "achieve in a performing art," to "write original works," and to "create artistic works." To "perform or compose music" was excluded because that option was not available after 1968. Table 7-2 indicates which goals fall under each broad heading. The four goals represented the dependent variables in separate regressions run for respondents from 1966, 1970, 1974, and 1978. Independent variables included personal and socioeconomic characteristics, type of institution attended, enrollment status, and major.

Artistic Goals

Adult women, younger adults, and adults from higher SES backgrounds (as measured by mother's education) were the most likely to have artistic aspirations. Sex differences regarding this goal decrease over time, and the SES effect gets stronger. The regressions indicate that those attending two-year colleges, particularly public ones, were less artistically motivated than other adults. This was also true of adults in Protestant four-year colleges in 1970 and 1974. On the other hand, adults in private liberal arts colleges (other than Protestant ones) were more artistically motivated than most other adults in college.

A causation problem arises when we attempt to interpret differences by type of institution attended. It might be that two-year colleges are unappealing to adults with artistic interests, and that if they improved course or program offerings in this area they could attract more students. Or maybe adults with artistic interests prefer the liberal arts college environment and so do not or would not take advantage of any artistically oriented programs two-year colleges might offer. Further analysis of these findings is needed.

Table 7-2
Correlates with Life Goals

Variable	Artistic 1966	Artistic 1970	Artistic 1974	Artistic 1978	Status 1966	Status 1970	Status 1974	Status 1978	Social 1966	Social 1970	Social 1974	Social 1978	Business 1966	Business 1970	Business 1974	Business 1978
Full-time		*	.059	-.029		*	.042	-.031		*	.041	-.034	*	*	.036	.059
Part-time	*	*	.017	-.020	*	*	.021	-.020	*	*		-.019	*	*	.025	-.025
First-time, full-time				-.048				-.091								
All two-year		-.056														
All universities										-.030						
Black colleges																
Public two-year	-.032		-.049		.063	.043	.076		.037	-.069	.062	-.082	.048	.041	.074	.026
Technical			*		-.039	-.085	-.045		-.115		-.078					
Public four-year	-.038		.018	.028		.038	*	.024	-.051		*	-.028				
Private four-year	.048		-.022			.026							.030	.030		
Protestant four-year																
Catholic four-year	-.031	-.031	.016	.032			.023				.024	.032	.047	-.027	-.033	-.022
Public universities																
Private universities																
Black public	.031				.029		.018		-.092							
Sex (female = 2)	.064	.041	.051	.027	-.234	-.219	-.087	-.100		-.030			-.235	-.189	-.112	-.098
Age	*	-.035	.033	-.046		-.044	-.021	-.047	*	-.047				-.062	-.043	-.070
Marital status (married = 2)		-.049	-.053	-.065		*										
White	.028	-.027	.054	.055	.045	-.036	-.018	.038	.044	.056	.079	-.031	-.039	-.076	-.030	-.028
Black	-.035		-.030			.051					.040	.021	.056	.045	.031	.075
Mother's education	.013	.024	.036	.021	.033	.031	.065	.066			.053	.048	.031	-.044	.048	.056
Agriculture	-.055	-.046	.015	.066			.109	.112			.085	.078			.046	.020
Biological sciences	.010	-.086	.051	.102	.049		.181	.242			.160	.210				
Business	-.062	-.062	.097		.064	.049	.085	.117	.066	-.035	.144	.168	.160	.124	.251	.305
Education	.124				-.019	-.029	.119	.154	-.042	-.040	.064	.091		-.066	.035	.039
Engineering					.071		.027	.038		-.050	.060	.070	.070		.098	.115
English		.053			-.019	-.026	.087	.098		-.090	.085	.105			.022	.030
Arts	.287	.274	.273	.286	-.003		.155	.196			.197	.227	-.042	-.042	.104	.120
Health	-.035	-.064	-.016	.033	.042		.078	.084		.062	.159	.160	.057		.036	.053
History	.032		.030	.082	.033	.031	.055	.056	.032		.108	.114		-.083	.050	.043
Humanities	.050		.067	.026	.066	-.026	.042	.028	.069		.022	.025	-.050	-.023	.021	.019
Math			.015				.071	.085		-.035	.047	.052		-.072	.017	.022
Physical science			*				*	.097			*	.088		-.025	.049	.069
Preprofessional					.051	.031	.138	.160	.050	.027	.220	.244	.109	-.028	.117	.078
Social science	.063	.047	.058	.059	.041	.056	.125	.136	.101	.080	.104	.107	.048	.048	.107	.106
Technical							.136	.138			.150	.159		-.081		.101
Nontechnical			.074	.080												
R^2	.1386	.1154	.1245	.1322	.0954	.0892	.0690	.0781	.0346	.0443	.0961	.0845	.1351	.1362	.0961	.1067

* = not available this year.

Blank = not significant.

1966 N = 5,981
1970 N = 7,819
1974 N = 17,392
1978 N = 12,479

Social Goals

This category refers to a set of activities concerned with helping others, and with political and social involvement to solve contemporary national problems. Although no differences were revealed by age or SES, white and black adults were more interested in these kinds of activities than other ethnic groups. These activities were relatively unimportant to adults who attended two-year colleges. Social science, health, and surprisingly, business majors (in the later seventies) were most interested in social goals. The variables included in the regressions did not differentiate much among adult students in their interest in social goals.

Business Goals

Although women were less interested in business ownership and being well-off financially than men were, these differences decreased over time. Younger adults had stronger aspirations regarding financial achievements, and blacks, particularly those in black colleges, had stronger aspirations than whites. Adults attending Protestant colleges were less likely than others to be concerned with business achievements.

As would be expected, business, engineering, and technical majors had the strongest business orientation; however arts majors also expressed relatively strong motivation in this regard.

Finally, we looked at differences between objectives of part-time and full-time adults in two years, 1974 and 1978 (see table 7-3). With a few exceptions, full-time adults were more likely to aim for all the goals on the list. However, the differences were not large enough that the overrepresentation of full-time adults affected the aggregate results described so far. Two objectives were more important for part-timers: "raising a family" and "having administrative responsibility for the work of others." The greatest difference was that part-timers were more interested in raising a family, which probably explains why they attended part-time. Many of the part-timers who were interested in having administrative responsibility for the work of others probably were attending college to gain promotions in their work. Full-timers were more interested in the more idealistic objectives.

As would be expected, adults who major in education, English, arts, history, and other humanities and social sciences are more likely than others to stress artistic achievements.

Less expected is the indication that in recent years biological and physical science majors were also more likely than others (for example, agriculture, business, engineering, health, and preprofessional majors) to seek achievement in the arts. Hence, it appears that institutions that allow

Table 7-3
Objectives Considered by Adult Respondents "Essential" or "Very Important," by Enrollment Status and Year
(in percentages)

	1974		1978	
	Part-time	*Full-time*	*Part-time*	*Full-time*
Becoming accomplished in one of the performing arts (acting, dancing, and so on)	7	10	7	11
Becoming an authority in my field	55	64	60	71
Obtaining recognition from my colleagues for contributions to my special field	35	41	37	46
Influencing the political structure	11	16	11	16
Influencing social values	29	35	31	36
Raising a family	66	58	70	61
Having administrative responsibility for the work of others	31	29	38	25
Being very well-off financially	41	41	48	47
Helping others who are in difficulty	61	67	66	71
Making a theoretical contribution to science	12	18	12	18
Writing original works (poems, novels, short stories, etc.)	10	15	12	17
Creating artistic work (painting, sculpture, decorating, etc.)	16	18	16	18
Being successful in a business of my own	30	37	33	40
Becoming involved in programs to clean up the environment	25	31	22	30
Developing a meaningful philosophy of life	66	72	67	70
Participating in a community action program	28	33	26	31
Keeping up to date with political affairs	37	41	31	39
Promoting racial understanding	—	—	36	44

science majors to take courses in the arts as well as the sciences may be attractive to adults in science fields. Science majors' interests in the arts may reflect the more diverse goals of students who begin or return to college after the traditional college-going years.

Status Goals

This category refers to scholarly accomplishment and leadership attainment. These objectives were more important to adult men than to adult women, although sex differences decreased over time. Young adults and blacks were more interested in status as defined here than were older people and whites. The racial difference was further emphasized by the fact that those who attended black colleges were more interested in status objectives than those who attended other kinds of institutions. Status was not important to adults who attended public two-year institutions.

In recent years adults in most of the major field categories had status goals (when compared with those undecided about their majors). The strongest major-status links were revealed among business, engineering, health, social science, technical, and nontechnical majors.

Summary

There were significant differences by sex and race in motivation to achieve life goals. Moreover, adults in two-year colleges were less motivated to achieve in any of the stated areas. If type of college can affect life goals, policies should be developed to encourage adults to attend four-year rather than two-year institutions. Then adults might develop stronger motivations to accomplish more for society and for themselves.

Cyril Houle, in *The Inquiring Mind* (1961), distinguishes three types of learning orientations: the goal-oriented, the activity-oriented, and the learning-oriented. Goal-oriented individuals are motivated by accomplishing clear-cut objectives, that is, vocational objectives. Activity-oriented individuals "take part because they find in the circumstances of the learning a meaning which has no necessary connection, and often no connection at all, with the content or the announced purposes of the activity" (p. 16). They may be motivated by loneliness, the desire to escape from a personal problem or an unhappy relationship or to complete a degree. And finally, the learning-oriented seek knowledge for its own sake. Learning for them is a way of life rather than a deliberate activity. Although Houle calls attention to the differences between these three learning orientations, he stresses that "no one of the three orientations is, after all, innately better than the others'' (p. 29). All of the adults are continuing learners. Differences among them are just a matter of the emphasis they place on the purposes and values of adult education.

Evidence of declining differences by sex in life goals leads us to infer that, over time, adult women who return to school will be seeking programs and services more similar to those men have sought in the past. For example, women probably will be more eager to enroll in academic courses rather than courses related to hobbies and other leisure activities. And black adults who return to college constitute a highly motivated group that may be an important source of new students in the future.

Implications: Accommodating New Clients

This book deals with the largest sample ever assembled of adults in college: 172,400 first-year students over the age of 21 who responded to the Cooperative Institutional Research Program's freshman survey between 1966 and 1978. Although the sample overrepresents full-time adults and four-year college students (as opposed to part-timers and two-year college students), we have presented findings so that differences between these groups can be discerned. In addition, we have made comparisons with a nationally representative sample of traditional-age students.

This chapter attempts to draw out some of the policy implications suggested by the data analysis. Although many of these recommendations are not new, our large-scale data base lends (or denies) support to what has been suggested. Our analysis was presented in six parts: demographics, college choice, the financing of college education, preparation for college, college plans, and life goals. The results presented in each chapter lead to a number of implications.

Because more and more adult women are returning to college, universities and colleges must find ways to facilitate their attendance. Many of these women are returning as part-timers. If part-timers generally get less out of college than full-timers, new approaches to part-time education will be needed so that these students can benefit as much as possible from the college experience. It is also important to determine whether barriers to the full-time attendance of adults, particularly women, exist and whether these barriers could be removed by explicit actions by institutions or at various levels of government. Specific institutions or programs that adults attend full time or from which part-time adults benefit highly should be identified and their characteristics should be isolated. Finally, whether these conditions can be transferred to other institutions should be considered. Some institutional barriers confronting all adult students, and women in particular, are: admissions procedures, university regulations and policies such as residence requirements, and especially financial aid (H. Astin 1976).

Increases in the attendance of married women in recent years suggest that some institutions have made it easier for women with traditional responsibilities to go to college. In-depth analysis would reveal whether day-care facilities, services such as transitional and counseling programs, or nontraditional course scheduling have facilitated this trend.

As the adult college population grows older, special consideration must be given to these students' needs. Colleges and universities that have effectively served people in their twenties are not necessarily the ones that will most effectively serve older students. Moreover, as older adults become interested in college attendance, admissions standards will have to be reevaluated. Many adults matriculate at open-admission, public institutions (The College Entrance Examination Board 1980). But for those who do not, high-school grades and test scores will probably not be very useful in determining their admissibility at moderately or highly selective institutions. Adjustments will have to be made for the fact that older people have lower grade-point averages because of grade inflation in recent years.

Because more and more of the adults in college have attended previously, colleges and universities must address the problems of transfer credits and the relevance of courses taken many years earlier. On the one hand, a college physics course taken in 1950 might only be equivalent to a high-school physics course today. Yet when courses can be equated, particularly in the humanities, for example, perhaps arbitrary time limits on credit should be removed. If the number of traditional-age college attenders is declining, then certain institutions, because of their need for students, may find it economically advantageous to require students to repeat courses that they have already taken. Colleges should resist such temptations; institutions that do not impose such requirements will certainly be more attractive to adults seeking degrees.

The proportion of minority-group members who enrolled in college was higher among adults than among traditional-age students. Yet many minority-oriented programs are aimed at traditional-age students. Institutions should identify exceptions to this generalization and evaluate the effectiveness of these programs.

If most adults select two-year colleges, the hopes expressed by four-year institutions that adults will make up for the declining number of college-bound 18-to-21-year-olds will be unfulfilled. The American Association for Community and Junior Colleges claims that adults want programs with a future and that the four-year college curriculum does not answer this need. Adults seek out two-year and community colleges because they are vocationally oriented. Two- and four-year colleges may be designed to meet different goals: for example, two-year colleges may be geared toward meeting immediate goals and four-year colleges toward meeting long-range goals.

Adults perceived a narrower range of choices available to them than did traditional students. The major constraints on adults were cost, location, and program. If a low-status institution is perceived by working adults to be all that is available, this may explain their low use of tuition remission programs. Hence higher-status institutions must make greater efforts to give their students financial aid and work opportunities. They may have to adjust the content, format, and scheduling of courses if they want to attract adult students.

While acknowledging that the most promising way to maintain enrollments for many institutions will be to identify and serve new kinds of students, Mayhew (1979) points out a number of dangers and pitfalls.

> The first of these dangers is that if new students are served on the campus itself, their very presence could so alter the character of the institution that, in the long run, it might lose its appeal to its traditional clients. Chatham College has created programs in management and communications for adult women that are quite popular. The proportion of total enrollment that is composed of these women has grown and could grow still larger. However, the women of traditional college age on campus have begun to resist the presence of larger numbers of older women on campus. Should that resistance intensify, it could produce an enrollment crisis in the group of women aged eighteen to twenty-two. For this reason, in all except the quite large institutions, programs for new kinds of students might better be conducted off campus, or at night, or in the summer, so that participants will not mingle with the traditional students. The charm of the idea of integrating new and traditional students and using underutilized classroom space and faculty time is offset by the dangers of changing, for the worse, the public image of the institution (p. 183).

Of course, there are other reasons to separate programs for adults from regular campus activities, in particular, to make them more convenient to adults in terms of time and location. In the late 1950s, during the debates over evening colleges, it was argued that adults benefited most from separate programs that could cater to their special needs (McMahon 1960). However care must be taken to prevent the downgrading of the educational experience by separating programs for adults. Tenured faculty may not want to teach off campus or at odd hours, or they may resist attempts to develop new curricula, even if enrollment declines are the alternative. Colleges may be tempted to hire adjunct or part-time faculty to teach adults off campus because they can pay them less, and this practice could seriously affect the quality of programs (Solmon, Ochsner, and Hurwicz 1979).

Another of Mayhew's (1979) cautions is particularly relevant to institutions attempting to cultivate a new adult clientele. He warns of misjudging the potential market for new programs. Because many adults are already attending college, more older people must be recruited to compensate for the declining pool of younger students, and these people may be harder to convince about the benefits of attending college. Since more high-school graduates have attended college since the 1960s than previously, college will lose some of its appeal for adults wanting to make up for previous disadvantage. Breneman and Finn (1978) caution, "because adult enrollments are vocationally driven, as the economic value of a college degree declines, as seems likely, motivation to earn the degree will also decrease'' (pp. 154-55). The long-term economic value of college degrees is still uncertain but it may improve. Thus, attempts to restructure institutions in order to attract adults must be worked out carefully.

Academic reputation was a very popular reason given by both adult and traditional-age students for selecting their particular colleges. This reason dominated both over time and across institutional types, which was surprising because adults most often attended two-year colleges, which are not usually academically superior to other kinds of colleges. Students might have been comparing their colleges with other nearby colleges with equally low, or lower, reputations, or their interpretations of ''good academic reputation'' could have been different from the interpretations used in many national ranking studies. Cross (1978) says: ''If that 'missing link' can be supplied [between learners and resources], the learning society can be a reality'' (p. 43). If this is true, colleges—particularly those that offer superior programs—should make special efforts to inform potential adult students of what they have to offer. For example, do adults know what choosing a nearby two-year college will mean to them in ten or fifteen years? Again, people affiliated with two-year and community colleges feel that national information on selectivity is not useful to adults because adults' sources of information on quality are very different from those used by traditional-age students. They believe that adults *know* the quality of local colleges and programs. Adult students just base their choice of college on different criteria than traditional-age students do.

Although we can list many barriers facing adults considering a return to college, probably the most interesting and complex ones involve finances. To understand the financial situation of adults, several issues must be addressed, particularly the true costs involved, the sources of funds available to adults, and the effects of financial constraints on their choices. Most adults base their decision to attend college on a different set of cost considerations than that used by students of traditional college age. If the adult is working, he or she may be forced to reduce time on the job and, unless paid educational leave is available, a reduction in income could result. Even high-level professionals may find their earnings reduced if, for example, they have to cut back on outside consulting activities to attend college. Athough it might be argued that 18-year-old high-school graduates also forego earnings if they attend college, the burden of this cost is probably greater for the older student who has fixed expenses (such as mortgage payments) which the younger student is unlikely to have. Adults with young children are also faced with the costs of child care when they must be away from home to attend classes. So it is important to know the extent to which adults delay entry or reentry into college until these costs are reduced (for example, when the children are grown and the house paid for).

Some observers argue that to maximize adult access to institutions of higher education, tuition should be kept as low as possible. Institutions must provide education at costs that both the students and society can afford (Boyer 1975; Fuller 1978), and per-course fees should be equalized for part-time and full-time students (Bishop and Van Dyk 1977; O'Keefe 1977) unless there are differences in the costs of providing the services.

Of course, if there were ways for adults to cover the costs of attending college, the burden of these costs would be reduced. And it might be argued that adults have more sources of support than do younger students, since more adults have jobs, the ability to borrow from banks, and years in which to accumulate savings.

The justification for subsidizing adults who attend college is complicated. If the benefits sought from college are private (that is, if they accrue only to the student and not to the larger society), many economists would argue that public subsidy is unwarranted. And most job-related benefits, as well as leisure-time or consumption benefits, are clearly private gains. If, however, a college education is considered a national right (that is, adults who were denied financial support earlier, when they would have been eligible, have a right to that aid later in life), or if the college education of adults is viewed as benefiting society (by increasing socioeconomic mobility, enhancing national productivity, and changing values, attitudes, and behavior in socially desirable ways), then the availability of financial aid to adults becomes a major concern.

Although most adult freshmen expressed at least some concern about financing their educations, part-time adult students were significantly less likely to express such concern than were those enrolled full-time. Not surprisingly, blacks and adults from poorer families had the most concern about financing their college educations, and adult women and younger adults (22-to-25-years-old) had more concern than men and older adults did.

The major sources adults used to finance their educations differed from those of traditional-age freshmen. Whereas traditional-age students relied on family aid and savings from part-time or summer employment, adults relied on personal savings, military benefits, or regular employment. Adult undergraduates were also much more likely than their traditional-age counterparts to borrow money to finance their educations.

Most adults must work to pay for college. Unless colleges at all levels, but particularly the four-year institutions, are willing to adjust to this need, their attractiveness to adult students will be limited. In particular, colleges will have to offer regular courses at times when working adults can attend. This factor is clearly important in explaining the appeal of community colleges for adults. However because work obligations may limit the impact of college on adults, the possibility of offering nonwork-related financial aid must be reconsidered.

Adults had better access to federal aid programs than we expected. Yet their higher basic living costs limit the effectiveness of aid programs, especially in terms of their choice of college and their persistence in college. The determination of need may have to be different for adults than for traditional students. It is important to know how adults would be affected by modifications in abiltity-to-pay calculations. One example is independent-student status: Should married students be able to declare themselves independent of their spouses for aid eligiblity?

GI Bill assistance has helped many adults returning to college. The effects of the declining availability of such aid must be further analyzed. Also, subsidized loan programs are more appealing to adults than to traditional students. The recent elimination of income limitations on certain loan programs may encourage adults to return to and remain in college. The effect of recent changes in eligiblity requirements for loan programs on adult attendance should be monitored carefully.

Specific proposals for financing the education of adults include turning the BEOG program into an entitlement program by allowing traditional-age students, who are eligible for financial aid but choose not to go to college immediately, to use the aid at any later point in life (Bishop and Van Dyk 1977). This proposal poses some problems. If BEOGs are provided to aid the needy, how can we justify their use by adults whose financial position has greatly improved since their teenage years?

Another problem is that students must attend college at least half time to qualify for BEOGs. Adults who attend less than half time are ineligible. Should this provision of the program be changed? The variation in institutional and federal definitions of less than full- or part-time status must also be addressed. Another question that remains unanswered is: Do adults receive less aid because they do not qualify for awards or because they do not know about programs for which they are eligible? If the problem is lack of information, some solutions are obvious.

So far, we have only touched on a major element in the financing of college by adults. Most financial aid policy assumes that adults who work have a revenue source to cover at least some, if not all, of their education expenses. However, if employed adults who return to school are accustomed to spending (or need to spend) most of their current earnings, then their normal salaries may not cover the additional expenses of education unless they change their living standards. For these people, the problem of finances may simply be one of increased demands on adequate financial resources, in which case something like a mortgage-payment deferment program might help. The unemployed, who may have serious financial problems, may be returning to school in the hope of improving their chances of employment, despite unemployment regulations which make college attendance illegal while one is collecting benefits. A related issue is independent-student status. A married person may not be able to use a spouse's earnings to pay for college. The question arises: How much of an adult's (or spouse's) salary can reasonably be considered as a source of funding for college?

Another set of issues regarding education-work links for adults involves who works at what and the impact of education choices. Only by comparing the nonattenders with adults in college can we see whether unemployed homemakers or working adults are more likely to attend. Other questions include: Is job level related to propensity to attend? Are men more likely to be working while in college than women are? What are the work experiences of adult students, including on-campus or off-campus jobs and number of hours worked? Do jobs constrain adults in their choice of institutions? Is the need to work a major reason for attending part-time? If so, do part-time attenders work full-time or part-time? What job-related differences are evident when part-time and full-time adult students are compared?

Perhaps the most vital set of issues related to the financing of education for working adults involves opportunities to participate in paid educational leave and tuition remission programs sponsored either by the employer or by a labor union (Charner 1980).

Burkett (1977) has suggested that organized education be subsidized by outside agencies such as state, national, and private philanthropic foundations; until now, most major efforts in this direction have come from the corporate sector. Other proposals for increasing adult participation in higher education include tax allowances (Boyer 1975; O'Keefe 1977) and a depreciation allowance for job obsolescence (London, Wenkert, and Hagstrom 1963). Tuition tax-credit proposals have not done well in Congress despite their popularity with various groups. However, most adults who already have access to employer-subsidized tuition remission plans have not taken advantage of them. Wirtz (1979) believes that such programs represent an economical way for employers to meet some of the costs of employee development. The programs would also be valuable to educational administrators concerned about current and prospective declines in enrollment. Therefore, he says, "there is both curiosity and concern about the apparent gap here between opportunity afforded and opportunity taken" (p. 2). Others have also observed that tuition aid is a significant "untapped resource" (Charner et al. 1978). Whether paid educational leave, which would eliminate or reduce costs of tuition remission programs, would be more attractive to prospective students is uncertain. And the willingness of many employers to develop such programs is questionable. In some cases, unions might be able to bargain for such fringe benefits, but the costs of these programs would be high.

Educational leave from jobs, or subsidization by employers, has also been suggested as a means of updating job skills, increasing worker morale, and so forth (Eide 1973; Sheats 1965). Of course, there is a difference between attending college and participating in formal or informal programs offered by employers. Many companies believe that they can provide relevant instruction at lower cost in-house than by sending workers back to school. The GI Bill of Rights for veterans confirms the positive effects of subsidizing educational undertakings. For example, subsidies substantially increased the college attendance of Vietnam veterans. Previously, men in the armed forces were less likely to attend college because many were already undergoing on-the-job training and the free correspondence schools available to them were not included in the census definition of school attendance. The question arises, however: Should a returning 21-year-old veteran who enlisted after high school and then went on to college after several years in the armed forces be viewed as an adult in college or as a slightly delayed traditional student?

Subsidization of both formal and informal educational activities by employers and others must be critically examined. If adults return to college for job advancement, the duration or persistence of the related benefits is important. The 50-year-old who returns to college for job advancement will benefit for only fifteen years or so. The teenager who goes to college will probably work for forty-five years or more. Hence, the benefit-cost ratio is higher for the younger person. As workers get older, their employers' incentives to subsidize their further education declines.

In other countries, employees often stay with one employer for their entire working careers, but in the United States, when an employer provides job-related training, workers tend to either demand salary increases or leave for other jobs. The lack of company loyalty discourages employer subsidization. Further study is necessary to determine what kinds of programs adults participate in (particularly those outside colleges) and to see whether those who participate in other training programs are more or less likely than others to be attending college.

In some ways, the value of returning to college with respect to job advancement depends on a person's field of study. The skills of engineers become obsolete more quickly than those of other kinds of workers. Thus their skills may need periodic retooling. But most engineers eventually move to administrative positions, so it might be less expensive for employers to hire recently graduated engineers than to send those with obsolete skills back to school. Perhaps engineers who need to update their skills should go back to business schools rather than engineering programs.

Some questions to be considered are: How prevalent are employer subsidies, paid educational leaves, and tuition remission? Similarly, to what extent do unions assist their members to return to college: Are workers in union-sponsored courses encouraged to take courses oriented toward union policies and activities? Does subsidization of educational activities by employers differ for older and younger workers? Does such subsidization depend on a person's field of study and occupation? Are differences in participation rates by age, field, and other variables attributable to differences in the employee's interest in or knowledge about the programs?

Finally, policymakers must know what proportion of working adults is eligible for employer subsidies. Why do many adults not take advantage of these programs? How many are uninformed about the programs available to them through their employers or unions? Is knowledge of or participation in such programs dependent on job or educational level or other personal characteristics? These are difficult questions to answer.

Adults who attend college are less well prepared than younger students. The only caveat here is that although adults responding to the CIRP surveys were more likely than traditional students to *say* that they were less well prepared and needed remediation, the two groups may not really differ. Perhaps both groups are poorly prepared, but the adults are more realistic; or perhaps adults are as well prepared but lack self-confidence.

Another avenue to pursue with respect to the relative preparation of adults and traditional-age students is to develop mechanisms for reality testing. Institutions should not rely on stereotypes or adults' own perceptions of how well prepared they are. Results of competency tests such as the Student Achievement Test (SAT) may be misleading, both because they may have built-in biases and because capable adults may not have had as much experience with these tests as recent high-school graduates have. Perhaps personal interviews coupled with recognition of the value of earlier experiences would facilitate assessment of the preparation and capabilities of older applicants. Nevertheless, remediation may be necessary just as careful evaluation of requirements, prerequisites, course loads, and course contents is necessary. Institutions may have to choose between attempting to bring adults up to generally accepted standards, and changing these standards to make them more consistent with the reasons adults are returning to college. There is some fear that changed standards will become lower standards. Although the changing of standards may be easier on students and more appealing to them in the short run, bringing adults up to accepted standards may yield greater payoffs over time. Also, as we have seen, adults indicated concern with program quality as a major factor in matriculation decisions, so lowering standards would be against the best interests of both the institution and its adult students. Adult degree programs and federal policies, are obviously not designed to create a two-tier structure for degree quality. Who should pay for the efforts to help poorly prepared adults in college is a vital economic and educational issue. But ignoring the problem of lack of preparation (if it does exist) will both limit adult enrollments and minimize the benefits for those who do attend.

A major factor in the college choice of adult students is that they must usually live at home. This situation may not be immutable: Adults might be willing to live on or near campus if subsidized housing were available to them. At present, however, most colleges cannot offer their adult students satisfactory housing. This is unfortunate given the evidence that traditional students benefit greatly from living on campus and that adult students who live in off-campus housing (other than their own homes) shoulder heavy financial burdens. As a result of their financial burdens, adult students are forced to attend colleges near their homes.

Because the degree aspirations of adults are somewhat lower than those of traditional students (perhaps because their goals are more specific or they are not seeking degrees), colleges must be chary in extrapolating the upper-division or graduate enrollments of adults from their attendance rates in the first year. Moreover, colleges should consider developing programs to raise the aspirations of returning adults. Despite their initial disadvantages in academic preparation or lack of self-confidence, some observers suggest that adult students are better prepared than their younger counterparts because they are motivated to make the effort and ready to work.

Most adult freshmen are in college to make up for previous disadvantages or to get ahead in their careers. Our data base does not include many members of the upper middle class who are pursuing leisure activities; this is indicated by the preponderance of students choosing majors and careers in business to the exclusion of the humanities, in particular. Moreover, the adult students in the HERI data base have life goals related to work and status rather than leisure. Humanities departments hoping to solve their declining enrollment problems by replacing younger students with adults should take particular note of this finding (Solmon, Ochsner, and Hurwicz 1979). Colleges hoping to recruit adults into any major and then to redistribute enrollment-based funds among departments must be prepared to expand their business programs. And companies should encourage employees to return to school to advance their careers rather than to pursue leisure activities.

Because most research on the impact of college and the value of a college education has concentrated on the traditional 18-to-22-year-old student, notions of good educational policy and practice are based on this group. We may have to revise these notions when evaluating higher education for adults, as is clearly demonstrated by the work of Alexander Astin. In *Four Critical Years* (1977), Astin concludes that (traditional-age) students get more out of college if they "get involved":

> The fact that most measures of student involvement are associated with greater-than-average changes in entering student characteristics supports the hypothesis that many changes after college entry may be attributed in part to the college experience rather than to maturation. For certain outcomes, student involvement is more strongly associated with change than either entering freshman characteristics or institutional characteristics.

There is, to be sure, some confounding of involvement with other factors. Students who live in college dormitories rather than at home, for example, tend to come from more affluent families and are more likely to attend four-year rather than two-year colleges. Nevertheless, involvement measures are strongly associated with many outcomes even after the effects of student and institutional characteristics are considered. Major findings for nine forms of involvement are summarized: place of residence, honors programs, undergraduate research participation, social fraternities, and sororities, academic involvement, student-faculty interaction, athletic involvement, involvement in student government, and verbal aggressiveness (p. 220).

Adults usually do not get as involved during college as traditional-age students do (particularly in nonacademic spheres). They live off campus rather than in residence halls. Many attend part time rather than full time. They get less nonreturnable financial aid, take out more loans, and work off campus rather than on campus. They do not usually participate in extracurricular activities, athletics, or student government. They do not get pledged to fraternities or sororities. And they rarely have as much time to interact with faculty as do students who are always on campus. Thus, some might argue that we must either accept the fact that they will benefit less from the experience, or we must effect changes in our institutions of higher education to facilitate adult involvement (McMahon 1960).

If the model of the traditional student is applied, adults appear to be deprived of important learning experiences and would not be expected to develop the same high motivation to benefit from college that younger, more involved students have. Hence they benefit less from college attendance. But why should the same model be used for adults and younger students? The former enter college with different goals and motives. Presumably, adults do not need college to help them mature. Adults make greater sacrifices to attend college than do recent high-school graduates. So it seems reasonable to assume that adults are less in need of the motivational benefits of involvement.

Adults are often very involved in the academic aspects of college. A recent study by C. Robert Pace (1979) confirms this view. He finds that adult students exert more effort than younger students in library use, classroom or course learning, faculty contact, writing, and scientific laboratory work, but less effort in a multitude of nonacademic or extracurricular activities. Adults attend college to maximize their academic and intellectual gains rather than to gain a "whole life experience." Yet adults report more impact ("gains") than traditional students do in intellecutal and personal development (Green 1980).

These arguments lead to the conclusion that efforts to restructure higher education so that adults can participate in the same ways traditional students do may be misdirected as well as costly and difficult to achieve.

Nevertheless, colleges should make some changes to facilitate adult access, choice, and persistence and to ensure that adults get the benefits they seek from the college experience.

These adaptations become particularly important when we recognize the alternative forms of education available to adults. It must be stressed that the HERI adult sample includes only those adult students not in extension programs, which may explain why certain stereotypes of returning adults are not confirmed here. However, in anticipating a huge flow of adults into traditional curricula, colleges must be aware that extension programs as well as informal learning settings of many types are their greatest competitors.

The education of adults can take many different forms. Harrington (1977) points out that there are differences between adult education, continuing education, and extension. According to Harrington, adult education serves "those who have completed or interrupted their schooling and are entering a college or university or are coming into contact with a higher education program after an interval away from the classroom" (p. xii). Continuing education, though often used as a synonym for adult education, is used by Harrington to refer to programs serving those returning to school to build on previous training. Extension refers to both formal and informal programs of higher education, but it differs from adult education in that it serves younger students as well as adults and is little used by private colleges and universities.

Other scholars do not distinguish between different types of education for adults. For example, Ziegler (1972) regards recurrent education as one possible future model for adult education. The Organization for Economic Cooperation and Development (1973) regards recurrent education as alternating incidental and lifelong learning with more organized and planned educational opportunities. Gass (1973) believes that recurrent education may be the best hope for connecting careers, education, and the economic system.

Some scholars make a distinction between education and learning (Organization for Economic Cooperation and Development 1973). They believe that learning is necessary for survival and that people learn in many situations. Education on the other hand, involves organized and structured learning activities confined to a planned situation. Therefore, although learning can be part of the lifelong learning movement, education cannot because it occurs only at a specific time and place. This distinction is questionable when applied to the adult population because adults are more likely than traditional-age students to learn or become educated at many different kinds of educational institutions. Most scholars view education as part of a broader endeavor within the framework of lifelong learning.

The education of adults takes place in a variety of ways and settings: for example, in formal colleges, through informal reading, and in courses offered by businesses, the military, the YMCA, churches, and so on (The Advisory Panel on Research Needs in Lifelong Learning During Adulthood 1978).

Much literature on the evening college movement was published during the late 1950s and early 1960s. Evening colleges are merely degree-granting colleges for part-time students (McMahon 1960). The obvious difference between evening colleges and other colleges is the time when the classes are held. Another characteristic of evening colleges is that they provide higher education for part-time adult students who must spend daytime hours in other pursuits. These people may or may not be seeking degrees. The evening college movement prevented higher education from becoming an economic class privilege in America.

Specific proposals for alternatives to formal adult educational programs include the extended campus, the special adult degree, individualized study, external degree programs, summer school, the educational passport, the continuing education unit (CEU), and provision of educational leave from jobs.

Schlaver (1977) describes many of these alternatives. The extended campus involves study outside the classroom under existing curricula that leads to a traditional degree. Adjustments for adult students are made in scheduling, residency requirements, and teaching style. The special adult degree involves programs where objectives, curriculum content, and methodology meet the special needs and interests of adults. Most of these programs provide a broad liberal arts rather than vocational or professional education. Individualized study involves making learning contracts that apply to work as well as to study. Under this arrangement, the institution sponsoring the individual specifies a minimum of general requirements. External degree programs evaluate knowledge acquired through experience rather than course work.

Summer school and the educational passport (Harrington 1977; Summerskill and Osander 1975) have been suggested as ways to augment the traditional educational opportunities available to adults in formal educational institutions. The educational passport is a record of achievements (that is, credentials for the educational world) that can be presented as a student moves through the educational system and the business world. Continuing education units (CEUs), discussed by Harrington (1977), have recently been introduced as a measure of participation in noncredit courses.

If they want to attract new adults to their programs, traditional colleges and universities must be aware of their competitors' efforts to educate older Americans. Three alternatives are open to them: They can make the necessary adaptations within their present systems (assuming that they know which changes are necessary); they can try to replicate what extension, noncollegiate, and informal learning settings offer; or they can do nothing and remain valuable only to those adults who can cope with their demands. The choice they make will determine the impact of adults on our colleges and of our colleges on adults.

Appendix A:
Supplementary Tables

Table A-1
Reasons Noted by Adult Male Respondents as "Very Important" in Selecting this College, by Marital Status, Year, and Sex
(in percentages)

	1975			1978		
	Unmarried	Married, Living with Spouse	Married, Not Living with Spouse	Unmarried	Married, Living with Spouse	Married, Not Living with Spouse
Relative/parent	6	4	7	5	2	9
Friend	11	11	14	10	9	14
Guidance counselor	6	5	5	5	4	6
Teacher	4	2	3	4	3	2
College representative recruited me	3	2	5	3	2	6
Opportunity to live away from home	6	1	6	—	—	—
Low tuition	28	31	33	18	20	25
Academic reputation of the college	43	40	49	46	42	45
Offered financial assistance	18	16	22	16	13	19
Special educational program offered	35	38	42	31	32	41
I was not accepted anywhere else	—	—	—	2	1	3
I wanted to live at home	11	25	13	10	26	16
Someone who had been here before advised me to go	16	17	20	16	14	21
I could not get a job	9	8	12	—	—	—
It will help me get a better job	57	65	70	—	—	—

Table A-2
Reasons Noted by Adult Female Respondents as "Very Important" in Selecting this College, by Marital Status, Year, and Sex
(in percentages)

	1975			1978		
	Unmarried	Married, Living with Spouse	Married, Not Living with Spouse	Unmarried	Married, Living with Spouse	Married, Not Living with Spouse
Relative/parent	6	6	7	4	4	6
Friend	12	11	15	12.	9	12
Guidance counselor	6	6	10	5	4	6
Teacher	4	3	4	4	2	4
College representative recruited me	3	2	4	3	2	4
Opportunity to live away from home	5	1	2	—	—	—
Low tuition	36	39	41	22	25	24
Academic reputation of the college	51	48	52	51	45	49
Offered financial assistance	26	14	30	23	12	32
Special educational program offered	49	50	54	43	43	46
I was not accepted anywhere else	—	—	—	2	1	1
I wanted to live at home	19	46	25	19	48	26
Someone who had been here before advised me to go	20	20	26	17	15	21
I could not get a job	11	8	17	—	—	—
It will help me get a better job	70	71	84	—	—	—

Table A-3
Financial Concern of Adult Respondents, by Marital Status and Year
(in percentages)

	1975			1978		
	Unmarried	*Married, Living with Spouse*	*Married, Not Living with Spouse*	*Unmarried*	*Married, Living with Spouse*	*Married, Not Living with Spouse*
No Concern	30	46	23	27	41	24
Some concern	40	36	37	42	40	41
Major concern	30	19	40	30	19	35

Table A-4
Financial Concern of Adult Respondents, by Year and Enrollment Status
(in percentages)

	1974		1978	
	Part-time	*Full-time*	*Part-time*	*Full-time*
No concern	58	35	47	28
Some concern	27	39	36	43
Major concern	15	26	17	29

Table A-5

Source of First Year's Educational Expenses for White Adult Respondents, by Type of Institution and Year

(in percentages)

	1974				1978			
	All Two-Year Colleges	All Four-Year Colleges	All Universities	All Black Colleges	All Two-Year Colleges	All Four-Year Colleges	All Universities	All Black Colleges
Parental, family aid, or gifts	18	29	29	16	13	21	25	21
Grants and scholarships								
Basic Educational Opportunity Grant	13	18	15	19	19	20	19	25
Supplemental Educational Opportunity Grant	5	7	6	6	5	6	7	7
College work-study grant	5	12	9	13	4	9	9	6
State scholarship or grant	8	16	11	11	8	13	14	12
College grant (other than above)	—	—	—	—	4	12	11	12
Local or private scholarship or grant	4	12	7	7	—	—	—	—
Other private grant	—	—	—	—	3	3	3	1
Loans								
Federally guaranteed student loan	8	20	17	1	7	16	16	2
National direct student loan	3	12	11	8	3	8	10	2
Loan from college	—	—	—	—	2	3	4	1
Other loan	5	9	7	3	2	3	5	4
Work and savings								
Part-time or summer work	37	52	55	48	—	—	—	—
Other part-time work while attending college	—	—	—	—	22	27	35	21
Full-time work while attending college	—	—	—	—	16	16	12	10
Full-time work	36	28	27	38	—	—	—	—
Savings from summer work	—	—	—	—	13	21	28	6
Personal savings	32	47	48	41	15	18	25	7
Spouse	35	31	29	35	23	18	18	19
GI benefits from your military service	41	39	40	39	17	16	18	14
Federal benefits from parent's military service	2	2	2	0	1	1	1	6
Parent's Social Security benefits	2	2	2	0	1	2	1	2
Other	10	11	10	12	6	7	6	4

Table A-6
Source of First Year's Educational Expenses for Black Adult Respondents, by Type of Institution and Year
(in percentages)

	1974				1978			
	All Two-Year Colleges	All Four-Year Colleges	All Universities	All Black Colleges	All Two-Year Colleges	All Four-Year Colleges	All Universities	All Black Colleges
Parental, family aid, or gifts	14	21	15	20	8	11	13	20
Grants and scholarships								
Basic Educational Opportunity Grant	39	41	49	29	43	52	54	41
Supplemental Educational Opportunity Grant	13	17	25	14	10	17	17	12
College work-study grant	11	24	21	18	10	16	15	14
State scholarship or grant	10	22	21	8	11	19	25	8
College grant (other than above)	—	—	—	—	6	14	12	4
Local or private scholarship or grant	7	12	20	7	—	—	—	—
Other private grant	—	—	—	—	3	5	2	3
Loans								
Federally guaranteed student loan	12	22	24	12	7	12	12	7
National direct student loan	9	14	23	10	6	9	11	6
Loan from college	—	—	—	—	2	4	4	3
Other loan	6	10	10	6	2	2	5	2
Work and savings								
Part-time or summer work	24	41	35	32	—	—	—	—
Other part-time work while attending college	—	—	—	—	15	13	15	14
Full-time work while attending college	—	—	—	—	18	14	13	19
Full-time work	45	43	33	46	—	—	—	—
Savings from summer work	—	—	—	—	5	10	11	10
Personal savings	18	31	17	27	4	6	6	7
Spouse	19	23	14	16	9	6	5	7
GI benefits from your military service	45	40	42	46	15	8	11	16
Federal benefits from parent's military service	5	4	2	3	2	1	2	2
Parent's Social Security benefits	5	5	3	2	2	2	1	2
Other	12	11	12	9	6	5	6	6

Table A-7

Source of First Year's Educational Expenses for "Other" Adult Respondents, by Type of Institution and Year (in percentages)

	1974				1978			
	All Two-Year Colleges	All Four-Year Colleges	All Universities	All Black Colleges	All Two-Year Colleges	All Four-Year Colleges	All Universities	All Black Colleges
Parental, family aid, or gifts	25	40	31	59	22	29	28	45
Grants and scholarships								
Basic Educational Opportunity Grant	24	41	39	27	22	35	41	14
Supplemental Educational Opportunity Grant	10	16	20	20	7	12	13	4
College work-study grant	11	26	28	23	6	11	14	7
State scholarship or grant	7	22	23	14	7	16	18	7
College grant (other than above)	—	—	—	—	4	12	16	5
Local or private scholarship or grant	6	19	20	17	—	—	—	—
Other private grant	—	—	—	—	5	6	4	5
Loans								
Federally guaranteed student loan	8	22	21	10	6	9	9	4
National direct student loan	4	10	24	5	4	8	10	4
Loan from college	—	—	—	—	2	2	4	2
Other loan	5	12	9	5	3	3	5	2
Work and savings								
Part-time or summer work	35	56	57	57	—	—	—	—
Other part-time work while attending college	—	—	—	—	20	19	28	15
Full-time work while attending college	—	—	—	—	18	9	6	12
Full-time work	46	30	20	39	—	—	—	—
Savings from summer work	—	—	—	—	12	15	25	10
Personal savings	28	42	44	46	10	12	15	8
Spouse	27	18	28	29	14	7	12	7
GI benefits from your military service	41	28	29	10	12	14	9	6
Federal benefits from parent's military service	5	5	2	0	2	1	1	6
Parent's Social Security benefits	4	2	4	0	1	1	1	0
Other	14	17	14	18	6	6	6	3

Table A-8
Source of First Year's Educational Expenses of Adult Respondents, by Year and Enrollment Status
(in percentages)

	1974		1978	
	Part-time	*Full-time*	*Part-time*	*Full-time*
Parental, family aid, or gifts	13	26	10	21
Basic Educational Opportunity Grant	7	26	9	30
Supplemental Educational Opportunity Grant	4	10	2	9
College work-study grant	3	13	2	10
State scholarship or grant	3	14	2	14
College grant (other than above)	—	—	2	10
Local or private scholarship or grant	3	9	—	—
Other private grant	—	—	2	3
Federally guaranteed student loan	5	17	3	13
National direct student loan	2	11	1	8
Loan from the college	—	—	1	3
Other loan	4	8	2	4
Part-time or summer work	19	50	—	—
Other part-time work while attending college	—	—	12	26
Full-time work while attending college	—	—	39	8
Full-time work	61	25	—	—
Savings from summer work	—	—	6	19
Personal savings	25	39	10	17
Spouse	34	27	23	15
GI benefits from your military service	29	45	9	17
Federal benefits from your parent's military service	2	3	1	1
Parent's Social Security benefits	2	3	1	2
Other	10	11	5	6

Table A-9

Source of First Year's Educational Expenses for Adult Respondents, by Marital Status and Year

(in percentages)

	1975			1978		
	Unmarried	*Married, Living with Spouse*	*Married, Not Living with Spouse*	*Unmarried*	*Married, Living with Spouse*	*Married, Not Living with Spouse*
Parental, family aid, or gifts	30	12	16	25	9	12
Grants and scholarships						
Basic Educational Opportunity Grant	27	14	42	30	14	44
Supplemental Educational Opportunity Grant	10	4	12	9	4	11
College work-study grant	12	5	13	11	4	10
State scholarship or grant	14	8	12	14	8	15
College grant (other than above)	—	—	—	10	6	9
Local or private scholarship or grant	8	5	6	—	—	—
Other private grant	—	—	—	3	2	4
Loans						
Federally guaranteed student loan	14	8	9	13	9	10
National direct student loan	10	5	10	8	4	7
Loan from college	—	—	—	4	2	3
Other loan	6	4	6	4	2	2
Work and savings						
Part-time or summer work	46	27	30	—	—	—
Other part-time work while attending college	—	—	—	28	17	16
Full-time work while attending college	—	—	—	14	16	13
Full-time work	28	29	27	—	—	—
Savings from summer work	—	—	—	23	8	6
Personal savings	40	26	20	18	13	7
Spouse	2	51	13	1	44	6
GI benefits from your military service	33	48	28	15	18	11
Federal benefits from parent's military service	2	2	2	1	1	1
Parent's Social Security benefits	3	1	3	2	0	2
Other	12	8	16	7	5	8

Table A-10

Source of First Year's Educational Expenses for Male Adult Respondents, by Marital Status and Year

(in percentages)

	1975			1978		
	Unmarried	*Married, Living with Spouse*	*Married, Not Living with Spouse*	*Unmarried*	*Married, Living with Spouse*	*Married, Not Living with Spouse*
Parental, family aid, or gifts	33	9	20	29	8	25
Grants and scholarships						
Basic Educational Opportunity Grant	21	14	21	24	18	24
Supplemental Educational Opportunity Grant	8	4	8	8	5	7
College work-study grant	11	5	8	11	5	13
State scholarship or grant	12	8	6	13	9	14
College grant (other than above)	—	—	—	9	6	9
Local or private scholarship or grant	7	4	5	—	—	—
Other private grant	—	—	—	3	3	7
Loans						
Federally guaranteed student loan	13	8	8	12	9	11
National direct student loan	8	4	11	7	5	5
Loan from college	—	—	—	3	2	3
Other loan	6	4	7	4	2	3
Work and savings						
Part-time or summer work	49	26	33	—	—	—
Other part-time work while attending college	—	—	—	29	20	14
Full-time work while attending college	—	—	—	14	26	17
Full-time work	26	36	33	—	—	—
Savings from summer work	—	—	—	27	11	13
Personal savings	43	23	20	18	14	9
Spouse	1	28	7	1	24	5
GI benefits from your military service	52	74	62	26	41	32
Federal benefits from parent's military service	3	4	4	2	2	2
Parent's Social Security benefits	2	1	1	2	1	2
Other	9	8	11	6	7	6

Table A-11

Source of First Year's Educational Expenses for Female Adult Respondents, by Marital Status and Year

(in percentages)

	1975			1978		
	Unmarried	Married, Living with Spouse	Married, Not Living with Spouse	Unmarried	Married, Living with Spouse	Married, Not Living with Spouse
Parental, family aid, or gifts	27	16	14	22	9	8
Grants and scholarships						
Basic Educational Opportunity Grant	35	15	52	35	13	51
Supplemental Educational Opportunity Grant	13	5	15	11	3	12
College work-study grant	15	4	15	12	3	9
State scholarship or grant	16	8	15	14	8	15
College grant (other than above)	—	—	—	10	5	9
Local or private scholarship or grant	9	6	7	—	—	—
Other private grant	—	—	—	3	2	3
Loans						
Federally guaranteed student loan	14	9	10	13	9	10
National direct student loan	12	5	10	10	4	7
Loan from college	—	—	—	4	2	3
Other loan	7	5	5	3	3	2
Work and savings						
Part-time or summer work	42	27	28	—	—	—
Other part-time work while attending college	—	—	—	28	15	16
Full-time work while attending college	—	—	—	15	11	12
Full-time work	31	20	24	—	—	—
Savings from summer work	—	—	—	19	6	4
Personal savings	36	30	20	16	13	6
Spouse	2	74	16	1	56	6
GI benefits from your military service	4	6	6	4	4	4
Federal benefits from parent's military service	1	1	0	1	0	0
Parent's Social Security benefits	4	1	3	2	0	2
Other	16	7	19	8	4	8

Table A-12
Source of First Year's Educational Expenses for Adult Respondents, by Father's Educational Attainment and Year
(in percentages)

	1975						1978					
	Grammar School or Less	Some High School	High School Graduate	Some College	College Degree	Post-graduate Degree	Grammar School or Less	Some High School	High School Graduate	Some College	College Degree	Post-graduate Degree
Parental, family aid, or gifts	15	17	21	28	41	48	13	14	17	21	29	38
Grants and Scholarships:												
Basic Educational Opportunity Grant	26	24	20	17	13	16	32	28	24	22	19	16
Supplemental Educational Opportunity Grant	11	9	7	8	6	6	9	7	8	8	6	5
College work-study grant	11	11	9	10	10	12	10	8	9	8	8	8
State scholarship or grant	11	11	12	11	10	13	12	13	12	13	10	11
College grant (other than above)	—	—	—	—	—	—	8	8	9	9	9	8
Local or private scholarship or grant	8	7	6	8	8	10	—	—	—	—	—	—
Other private grant	—	—	—	—	—	—	4	2	3	3	3	3
Loans:												
Federally guaranteed student loan	13	14	13	15	14	17	9	11	12	13	14	12
National direct student loan	8	8	8	9	7	10	7	5	8	8	7	6
Loan from college	—	—	—	—	—	—	2	3	3	4	3	3
Other loan	7	6	7	6	6	8	3	3	3	4	3	4
Work and Savings:												
Part-time or summer work	36	40	43	48	53	56	—	—	—	—	—	—
Other part-time work while attending college	—	—	—	—	—	—	18	22	25	28	30	27
Full-time work while attending college	38	36	34	35	30	28	15	16	17	15	12	9
Full-time work	—	—	—	—	—	—	—	—	—	—	—	—
Savings from summer work	—	—	—	—	—	—	11	14	18	21	25	23
Personal savings	28	32	37	42	48	48	11	13	17	21	25	22
Spouse	29	30	28	29	26	28	16	18	19	18	14	13
GI benefits from your military service	43	44	43	36	33	28	15	16	18	16	14	13
Federal benefits from parent's military service	3	3	2	2	2	2	1	1	1	1	1	1
Parent's Social Security benefits	3	2	2	2	2	4	2	2	1	1	1	2
Other	12	10	10	10	12	12	7	7	6	6	6	5

Table A-13
Probable Major of Adult Respondents, by Marital Status and Year
(in percentages)

	1975			1978		
	Unmarried	*Married, Living with Spouse*	*Married, Not Living with Spouse*	*Unmarried*	*Married, Living with Spouse*	*Married, Not Living with Spouse*
Agriculture	2	2	1	2	1	1
Biological sciences	5	3	3	4	2	3
Business	16	21	19	19	22	22
Education	7	9	6	7	9	8
Engineering[a]	6	6	4	8	5	3
English	2	2	2	2	2	1
Health professional	13	17	19	13	20	19
History and political science	4	2	2	3	1	2
Humanities	4	4	2	3	3	2
Fine arts[a]	7	4	4	8	4	4
Mathematics and statistics	1	0	1	1	0	0
Physical sciences	2	2	1	2	1	1
Preprofessional[b]	—	—	—	2	2	1
Social science	11	8	14	9	9	13
Other fields (technical)[a]	9	10	10	8	8	12
Other fields (nontechnical)[a]	9	9	8	8	7	7
Undecided	3	2	2	2	2	2

[a]In 1978 the category of fine arts included architecture and the category of other fields (technical) included other professional. In 1975, fine arts was included in the engineering category and other professional was included in other fields (nontechnical). These four majors are therefore not directly comparable across the two years.

[b]The category of preprofessional major was not available in 1975.

Appendix B:
1977 Follow-Up of the
1970 Freshman Cohort

To gain more insight into the collegiate experiences of adult and traditional-age students, we analyzed a subsample of respondents to the HERI-administered 1977 follow-up of the 1970 freshman cohort. The various follow-up surveys issued by HERI (with the support of a number of different funding agencies) include posttests of freshman survey items and items specific to the interests of the sponsoring group(s).[1]

From the 28,599 questionnaires that were sent to the 180,000 CIRP respondents of 1970, a sample of 9,039 students was drawn for the current analysis. Of the 9,039 respondents on which this analysis was based, only 134, or 1.5 percent, of the respondents were classified as adults when they were college freshmen in 1970. Because the sample of adults available for analysis is quite small and the respondents were randomly selected and not necessarily representative of all those who responded to the 1970 survey, the results cannot be generalized to all adults in postsecondary education.

In addition to providing preliminary longitudinal analysis of this subgroup of adults, the 1977 follow-up data allow us to examine career outcomes. The information yielded from such an analysis also shows the possibilities of building on current work by resurveying cohorts or adults who attended college and responded to the CIRP survey when they were freshmen.

The Decision to Enter College

According to the follow-up data, the primary reason that freshmen attend college is to get a better job (see table B-1). At least 70 percent of both those who were of traditional age and those who were over 21 when they entered college cited this reason as very important. Getting a better job was much less likely to be a consideration for single students than for married ones; the exception was older single women, who were more likely to cite this reason than were older married women. It would seem, then, that institutions wishing to attract either more traditional students or more adult students should emphasize students' career development rather than their personal, intellectual, and social development.

The next most common reasons given for attending college—cited by 50 percent or more of both groups—were to learn more about their interests, to gain a general education, to make more money, and to improve their

113

Table B-1

Very Important Factors in Decision to Attend College, by Age

(in percentages)

	Under Age 22	Age 22 or Over
To prepare for graduate or professional school	16	19
To improve academic abilities	54	52
To contribute more to my community	17	21
To get a better job	75	70
To make more money	55	57
To gain a general education and appreciation of ideas	61	63
To learn more about things that interest me	70	70
To meet new and interesting people	40	18
To get involved in extracurricular college activities	11	4
To be with friends	10	2
To find a spouse	2	1
To avoid the draft	5	0
Parental or family encouragement	33	10
Nothing better to do	5	2
Always expected to go	42	14
N	8,824	729

academic abilities. Learning about topics of interest and gaining a general education and appreciation of ideas were more important to women than to men and to the older respondents, especially if they were single, than to the younger. The women who responded to the follow-up survey were more interested in improving their academic abilities than the men were, especially if they were older and married. Married women cited this reason more often than single women, and single men cited this reason more often than married men. The men surveyed were more concerned than the women with making more money. Making more money was given as a reason for entering college more often by older respondents and those who were married, but 62 percent of the older single women cited this reason as compared with 52 percent of the older married women. Only about 20 percent of both the older and younger respondents said that preparing for graduate or professional school was a very important reason in their decision to attend college.

"Although it was important to many freshmen to go to college for general academic reasons, it was at least as important, if not more so, to attend in order to improve their chances in the job market" (Ochsner 1979, p. 12). Very few of those who were adults as freshmen, as compared with those who were of traditional college age, decided to attend college because they wanted to be with friends, or get involved in extracurricular activities, because of parental or family encouragement, or because they were expected to go. More than twice as many of the younger respondents than older ones said that the prospect of meeting new and interesting people played a significant part in their decision making. This reason was especially important to the younger women and to all single respondents.

Tuition is another factor that affects the decision to attend college. Those who were adults when they were college freshmen in 1970 attended less expensive colleges than did their younger counterparts (see table B-2). Most of the older respondents (57 percent, as compared with only 25 percent of the younger) spent $500 or less on tuition in 1970. Forty-four percent of those who were younger as freshmen spent from $500 to $1,000 on college tuition, while only 24 percent of the older respondents spent this much.

Adult students may make more money (for example, from full-time work) than younger students do, but they may not be able to allocate as much of their earnings to pursuing a college education. Many adult students, therefore, attend two-year colleges. Two-year colleges have lower tuitions but are relatively nonselective and may be lower in quality than four-year colleges and universities. Costs then are a real concern to adult students. Four-year institutions will have to either lower tuitions, provide more financial aid, or make the financial aid that is available more attractive if an adult clientele is to make up for the declining number of 18-to-21-year-olds and if the adults' college experiences are to be of high quality.

Academic Attainments

Most college freshmen followed up in the 1977 survey reported grade-point averages between B and C+ for their undergraduate years, with older respondents more likely than younger respondents to fall into this category.

Table B-2
Tuition of College for 1970 Freshmen, by Age
(in percentages)

	Under Age 22	Age 22 or Over
$250 or less	8	27
$250-$499	17	30
$500-$999	44	24
$1,000-$1,499	6	8
$1,500-$1,999	8	8
$2,000-$2,499	9	3
$2,500-$2,999	7	1
$3,000-$3,499	2	0
$3,500 or more	0	0
N	8,905	134

A substantial proportion of the traditional-age freshman population (36 percent) reported A, A − , or B + grade-point averages.

Although adult students came to college feeling less prepared than their traditional-age counterparts, this perceived lack of preparation did not seem to hamper their ability to perform almost as well in their college courses as those who were younger and supposedly better prepared. Perhaps, then, adults do lack self-confidence in facing a new and somewhat threatening environment populated primarily by younger people. If lack of self-confidence is a problem, a freshman orientation session to reassure adult students of their capabilities and to ease their fears might be a wise investment of time and money.

The younger students' initial degree aspirations were higher than those of their adult counterparts (see table B-3). More of the adults than traditional-age students who pursued an associate of arts degree or its equivalent in 1970 actually attained only this goal by 1977 (67 percent of the adults versus 43 percent of the traditional-age students). Clearly, younger students with this initial aim went on for at least a bachelor's degree. Younger students aspiring to a bachelor's or advanced degree were more likely to have obtained such a degree, with the exception of the master's degree, whereas a slightly higher proportion of adults who planned on receiving this degree actually obtained it (17 percent of the older students versus 14 percent of the younger students). Therefore, more of the adult students were underachievers (48 percent, as compared with 39 percent of their younger counterparts) as far as meeting their initial goals was concerned. A larger percentage of the younger students actually attained their original goals, but about equal numbers of both groups were overachievers in that they attained higher degrees than those they originally sought (8 percent of both groups).

One explanation of the lower attainment of the adult students is that they merely had not yet completed the courses of study required to obtain the degrees they intended by 1977 because they were attending part-time. Another explanation is that the degree aspirations of the adults in the follow-up sample might have actually been lower than those of younger students because many of them attended college for vocational reasons, that is, to advance in their careers or to make midlife job changes. So they may have sought only the minimum college education needed to reach these goals. Although traditional-age freshmen may have been too young and unsettled to know exactly what they were seeking, they did know that the baccalaureate was the minimum needed for a desirable entry-level position in the labor force. They were not committed to, nor did they have objections to, getting a higher degree. Career counselors could be of help to younger freshmen by providing accurate information on the degree requirements for various jobs.

Table B-3
Highest Degree Planned When Entered College, by Highest Degree Held in 1977 and Age
(in percentages)

Highest Degree Planned When Entered College	Highest Degree Held by Those under Age 22						Highest Degree Held by Those Age 22 or Over					
	None	A.A.	B.A	M.A	Ph.D.	Other	None	A.A.	B.A.	M.A	Ph.D.	Other
None	31	9	43	10	1	5	—	—	—	—	—	—
Associate or equivalent	21	43	32	1	0	4	0	67	20	0	0	13
Bachelor's	11	6	74	7	0	2	22	21	56	0	0	2
Master's	8	4	71	14	1	1	0	17	61	17	0	6
Doctorate or equivalent advanced, professional (Ph.D., M.D., D.D.S., D.V.M., LL.B.)	8	3	64	20	4	1	8	8	58	25	0	0
Other	19	6	62	6	0	6	—	—	—	—	—	—

Selection of an Undergraduate Major

"The reasons students go to college may not be as important to college academic and career counselors as the reasons they choose their particular major fields. Certainly college counselors cannot have much impact on how or why freshmen have already decided whether or not to go to college and which colleges they wish to attend. That is the responsibility of high school counselors, and to some extent, college recruiters. College counselors can, however, influence students' selection of major fields or at least their selection of curricular paths" (Ochsner 1979, p. 12).

Whatever their ages when they matriculated in 1970, seven years later most respondents said that a very important factor in their selection of an undergraduate major was that it would give them a better chance to get a meaningful job (see table B-4). However, those who were 22 or over as freshmen were more likely to cite this reason than younger students. Intellectually challenging subject matter and a special aptitude for the subject were also important considerations, especially for those of traditional college age in 1970.

In summary, students seem to choose their undergraduate majors for the same reasons they attend college. The primary motivating forces were a

Table B-4
Very Important Factors in Selecting Undergraduate Major as Reported in 1977, by Age
(in percentages)

	Under Age 22	Age 22 or Over
Greater breadth than other disciplines	22	16
Better chance to get higher paying job	23	40
Better chance to get meaningful job	53	64
Intellectually challenging subject matter	50	43
Peer group influence	4	4
Special aptitude for subject	52	36
Faculty advice, encouragement	12	11
Family advice, encouragement	13	14
Encouragement by person in field	14	15
Better chance of admision to graduate or professional school	9	12
No better alternative	9	5
Easy subject	3	1
Quickest way to graduate	3	3
N	8,627	124

desire for intellectual development and concerns about the job market. Only about 10 percent of the respondents were influenced in their choice of major by the possibility of increasing their chances of admission to graduate or professional school.

College Counseling

Those who were adults when they entered college in 1970 were slightly more receptive than their younger counterparts to the various kinds of college counseling (academic, career, and personal) offered (see table B-5). They were particularly receptive to personal counseling. Although not shown in table B-5, the data indicated that personal counseling was especially popular among single adult men and married adult women. Probably, personal counseling helped adult students cope with the fear associated with adjusting to a new and predominantly youth-oriented environment. Also, older students may have been more aware of the value of a free service. For both age groups, academic counseling was used most, followed by career counseling and then personal counseling. Perhaps personal counseling was used least because there is more stigma attached to it than to the others.

Most of the respondents were generally satisfied with the different kinds of college counseling they received. However, many of the younger respondents were not satisfied with the career counseling available to them (see table B-6). Only about 15 percent of the younger respondents and 25 percent of the older respondents who received college counseling indicated that they were very satisfied with it. Clearly, the quality of college counseling services needs to be improved. Moreover, many students (especially those of traditional college age) never sought counseling services, and an overwhelming majority of those who received it came away dissatisfied.

Satisfaction with College Experiences

Almost three-quarters of those respondents who were of traditional college age in 1970, but only 61 percent of the older group, stayed in their original colleges during their entire undergraduate careers (see table B-7). Adult students were more likely to have attended at least two colleges (48 percent of the older respondents versus 38 percent of the younger respondents). This does not necessarily mean, however, that older respondents were less satisfied with their college experiences. In fact, although the majority of the respondents were very satisfied with the colleges they attended, adults tended to be more satisfied than their younger counterparts. Approximately 60 percent of the older respondents said they were "very satisfied" as compared with about 50 percent of the younger respondents (see table B-8).

Table B-5
Types of College Counseling Received, by Age
(in percentages)

	Under Age 22	Age 22 or Over
Academic or course counseling	86	87
Career counseling	68	73
Personal counseling	52	62
N	8,905	134

The population of older students who attended more than one college was probably made up of adults who began their college careers at two-year colleges and then transferred to four-year institutions. Most traditional-age college freshmen selected four-year colleges and universities to begin with.

If they were to attract new adults to their programs, four-year colleges and universities must be aware of their competitors' efforts to educate older Americans. Two-year colleges already seem to be appealing to the vocational interests of adult students.

When questioned about the usefulness of a college education, the majority of both groups said the most important benefit was that it increased their general knowledge (see table B-9). This was true regardless of sex or marital status.

Younger respondents of both sexes and older women were more likely than older men to indicate that they learned a skill in college that enabled them to get their first jobs and that having a baccalaureate was a factor in their being hired by their current employers. More of the older respondents, especially the married women, said that a college education was beneficial in that it increased their chances of finding a good job. Again, intellectual and job-connected benefits were the primary considerations.

Table B-6
Satisfaction with Types of College Counseling Received, by Age
(in percentages)

	Academic or Course Counseling		Career Counseling		Personal Counseling	
	Under Age 22	Age 22 or Over	Under Age 22	Age 22 or Over	Under Age 22	Age 22 or Over
Not satisfied	42	30	56	43	39	42
Somewhat satisfied	45	42	35	36	45	30
Very satisfied	13	28	9	22	16	28
N	7,554	112	5,978	93	4,519	81

Table B-7
Whether or Not 1970 College Was the Same as the Last College Attended, by Age
(in percentages)

	Under Age 22	Age 22 or Over
No	27	39
Yes	73	61
N	8,795	130

Younger respondents, especially married men, were much more likely to say that their college education increased their desire to travel and taught them how to get along better with people. Older respondents were probably specifically concerned with the effects of a college education on their job opportunities and their career advancement; younger respondents were also interested in becoming well-rounded people. For example, 54 percent of those who were adults when freshmen agreed that the chief benefit of a college education was that it increases one's earning power, as compared with only 39 percent of those who were of a traditional college age when they were freshmen (see table B-10). By 1977 however many of the younger respondents agreed somewhat with this statement (see table B-11).

If they had it to do over again, only about a quarter of the sample said they would probably attend different institutions (see table B-12). Approximately 30 percent said there was a very good chance that they would change their major fields. The greatest proportion of the younger respondents (47 percent) said that if they were considering college today, with their present knowledge and experience, the major change they would make would be to take more courses in a different subject area. Only 36 percent of the older respondents said that there was a very good chance that they would make

Table B-8
Satisfaction with Colleges Attended, by Age
(in percentages)

	Under Age 22		Age 22 or Over	
	College Entered in 1970	Last College Attended	College Entered in 1970	Last College Attended
Not satisfied	12	8	8	2
Somewhat satisfied	36	41	33	40
Very satisfied	52	51	59	58
N	8,740	2,373	129	50

Table B-9
Usefulness of a College Education, by Age
(in percentages)

	Under Age 22	Age 22 or Over
Learned a skill that enabled me to get my first job	39	30
Increased my chances of finding a good job	50	58
Helped me choose my life goals	34	36
Gave me knowledge and skills that I use in my current job	44	50
Bachelor's degree a factor in being hired by current employer	45	38
Bachelor's degree necessary for promotion	32	29
Contacts with professors or friends helped me get my current job	14	13
Increased general knowledge	68	72
Increased ability to think clearly	51	51
Increased leadership ability	32	34
Increased critical thinking or analytical skills	54	50
Improved self-discipline and ability to follow rules	34	35
Improved self-confidence	44	43
Increased perseverance	36	35
Increased creativity	30	34
Improved writing ability	32	39
Increased insight	46	46
Increased cultural perspective	44	40
Taught me how to get along better with people	36	28
Increased political awareness	24	28
Increased desire to travel	32	21
N	8,849	126

this change. More than a third of both age groups said they would change or broaden the range of their career goals. The changes that both age groups said they would make seem to have involved a realistic assessment of the employment situation at the time. In 1977, when many of these students were in the labor force, they probably realized either that they had chosen the wrong major to fulfill their career aspirations or that by concentrating on just one academic area or one career goal, they had limited themselves as far as other career options were concerned.

Younger respondents were more likely than older respondents to say

Table B-10

Attitudes toward the Statement, "The Chief Benefit of a College Education Is that It Increases One's Earning Power," by Age

(in percentages)

	Under Age 22	Age 22 or Over
Disagree strongly	25	19
Disagree somewhat	35	28
Agree somewhat	33	42
Agree strongly	6	12
N	8,750	131

that if they were considering college with their present knowledge and experience, they would change some social experience. The explanation for this difference may be that, because younger students are generally more interested in the social life of the college, they are also more likely to regret not having taken advantage of some of the social opportunities or experiences offered to them.

Very few of the respondents (5 percent) said that they would not attend college at all. A larger proportion of older respondents (22 percent) than younger respondents (16 percent) said that the chances were excellent that they would do it all the same way again.

Employment While in College

Most students, regardless of their age as freshmen, worked part-time for certain periods while they were in college (see table B-13). Part-time employment was more characteristic of traditional-age students and those who were single adults when freshmen. On the other hand, full-time employment during the entire undergraduate career was much more characteristic of adults (23 percent) than of traditional-age students (2 percent). Younger respondents were much more likely to have held at least one job on campus (40 percent of the younger respondents versus 16 percent of the older respondents), which probably reflects their greater involvement in college life.

Greater flexibility in the scheduling of classes is needed to accommodate students who work at least part-time while attending college. Scheduling adjustments by colleges and universities are particularly critical for adults who, for example, are employed full-time and have family-related responsibilities.

Table B-11
Change in Attitude from 1970 to 1977 toward the Statement, "The Chief Benefit of a College Education Is that It Increases One's Earning Power," by Age
(in percentages)

| | 1977 | | | | | | | |
| | Under Age 22 | | | | Age 22 or Over | | | |
1970	Disagree Strongly	Disagree Somewhat	Agree Somewhat	Agree Strongly	Disagree Strongly	Disagree Somewhat	Agree Somewhat	Agree Strongly
Disagree strongly	29	13	7	6	28	6	2	0
Disagree somewhat	29	27	20	17	12	19	11	7
Agree somewhat	34	46	52	47	40	58	66	60
Agree strongly	9	13	21	30	20	17	22	33
N	2,218	3,054	2,914	564	25	36	55	15

Table B-12
Changes Would Make if Considering College Today (with Present Experience and Knowledge), by Age
(in percentages)

	Under Age 22	Age 22 or Over
Change specialization within field	30	22
Change major field	33	30
Change some social experience	31	22
Change institution	25	28
Change or broaden range of career goals aspired to	40	38
Not attend college	4	35
Take more courses in another area	47	36
Plan to go to graduate school in undergraduate field	24	27
Work for an advanced or professional degree in another field	24	24
Do it all the same way	16	22
N	8,430	124

Choosing a Career

A college career counselor usually has the most contact with students during their senior years, when they become seriously concerned with career planning. But by that time it is often too late. At least three-quarters of both the older and younger respondents in our sample had already chosen their careers by the time they were seniors (see table B-14). In fact, 50 percent of those who were adults when college freshmen and 34 percent of those who were of traditional-age said they had chosen their careers before they even entered college. The former group probably made their career decisions early because they were older and already employed in full-time jobs and had come to college to learn the skills required for job advancement or career change. Only 25 percent of the younger respondents, but 38 percent of the older respondents, thought that students should make their career decisions before entering college. More of the older respondents probably felt this way because they had had time to experiment with different jobs and thus to decide on their careers before entering college. Many of the adult students who made career decisions early in their undergraduate years later came to feel that a student's career choice should not be made too early. Nonetheless, at least 80 percent of both groups advocated choosing a career before the senior year. Career counselors should therefore be

Table B-13
Employment while in College, by Age
(in percentages)

	Under Age 22	Age 22 or Over
Held one job on campus as a undergraduate	24	13
Held more than one job on campus as an undergraduate	16	3
Held one job off campus as an undergraduate	28	31
Held more than one job off campus as an undergraduate	24	20
Worked full time all the time attended college	2	23
Worked full time for certain periods while in college	28	26
Worked part time all the time attended college	19	15
Worked part time for certain periods while in college	49	31
N	8,905	134

available to students before the senior year, and greater efforts should be made to assure that students make fuller use of career counseling services.

Successful Job Search Methods

Most of the respondents who were employed full time in 1970 had obtained their current jobs through direct personal application to the employer (see table B-15). College placement offices, professional contacts, contacts from a previous job, parents, relatives, friends, and luck or chance were more helpful to younger respondents; civil service application was a more effective method for older respondents.

Table B-14
When Made Career Choice, by Age
(in percentages)

	Under Age 22	Age 22 or Over
Before entering college	34	50
Upon entering college	7	8
At the time major must be selected	9	8
During college, before senior year	22	18
During senior year	6	2
At graduation	1	1
Within two years after graduation	11	7
More than two years after graduation	4	6
At present time (within last few months)	5	1
N	8,486	120

Table B-15
Job Search Methods that Worked in Getting Current or Most Recent Job, for Full-Time Employees, by Age
(in percentages)

	Under Age 22	Age 22 or Over
College placement office	11	5
College professors	5	5
Public/state employment service	4	7
Civil service application	5	18
Private employment agency	6	6
Recruiting teams from government, industry	3	1
Professional contacts	13	7
Direct personal application to employer	48	52
Professional organizations, meetings	1	1
Newspaper advertisements	8	11
Professional journals, periodicals	1	1
TV, radio	0	0
Other advertising	1	1
Community action/welfare groups	0	1
Registration with a union	0	0
Met new employer through previous job	6	1
Unsolicited offer	5	1
Parents/other relatives	10	5
Friends	17	12
Luck/chance	17	12
N	5,680	85

Only 11 percent of the younger respondents and 6 percent of the older respondents successfully used college placement offices to get their current or most recent jobs. This difference suggests either that adult students are not as likely as their younger counterparts to take advantage of the services offered by their colleges or that college placement offices are not geared toward meeting the needs of an adult clientele.

Current Occupation

Of those who were adults when they entered college in 1970, 42 percent were employed full time in an occupation that fell into the unspecified "other" category (see table B-16). Research scientist was the most frequently mentioned full-time occupation for traditional-age freshmen (35 percent). Businessman was the second most common occupation among both groups. A relatively large proportion of the older group (8 percent, versus 3 percent of the younger) were nurses.

Table B-16
Current Occupation of Full-Time Employees, by Age
(in percentages)

	Under Age 22	Age 22 or Over
Artist (including performer)	4	0
Businessman	22	24
Clergyman	0	0
College teacher	1	1
Doctor (M.D. or D.D.S.)	0	0
Education (secondary)	8	6
Elementary teacher	11	11
Engineer	6	5
Farmer or forester	2	1
Health professional	5	3
Lawyer	1	0
Nurse	3	8
Research Scientist	35	0
Other choice	0	42
Undecided	3	0
N	6,109	101

Relation of Job to Major

At least 50 percent of both groups of respondents who were employed full time when the follow-up was conducted were working in jobs closely related to their major fields (see table B-17). Those who were working at full-time jobs only somewhat or not at all related to their undergraduate majors would have preferred jobs in their fields: Forty-two percent of the younger respondents and 26 percent of the older respondents indicated that employment opportunities were scarce in jobs related to their majors, a reason that takes much of the responsibility out of the individual's hands (see table B-18).

Most of the reasons specified on the follow-up questionnaire were given more often by younger respondents: "never planned to take a closely related job," "prefer work not closely related," "found job that offers a better chance of career advancement," "related jobs not available where I live and do not want to move," and "could not get a closely related job, but would prefer one." On the other hand, more older respondents said that they were working in a job that was unrelated or only somewhat related to their undergraduate major because they had found a better-paying job or because their job options were limited by their spouses' circumstances and by family responsibilities.

Table B-17
Relation of Current or Most Recent Job to Undergraduate Major, for Full-Time Employees, by Age
(in percentages)

	Under Age 22	Age 22 or Over
Not related	30	29
Somewhat related	20	19
Closely related	51	52
N	6,284	101

Contributon of Various Experiences to Job

The experiences or training that contributed a great deal to the current or most recent jobs of the respondents were general on-the-job experience, particular course(s) in major field, and college study in general (see table B-19). Younger respondents were somewhat more likely to mention these experiences than older respondents.

The older respondents were more likely to feel that formal training, or courses outside their college programs, and programs offered by their employers contributed significantly to their current jobs; their younger counterparts felt that formal traning programs at their places of employment were an important contribution to their current jobs.

Job Characteristics

Various characteristics of jobs influence satisfaction and dissatisfaction. These characteristics include utilization of skills, status or prestige, salary, degree of responsibility, job level, and autonomy.

Because the older respondents had been in the labor force longer, one would expect them to hold higher-status positions and to have more responsibility in their jobs than their younger counterparts. Surprisingly, more younger than older respondents said they were working at a professional level and that they had policy- and decision-making responsibilities (see table B-20). This implies that entry-level workers interpret the meaning of the term "professional level" differently than the experienced workers. About half of all the respondents felt they had sufficient status or prestige in their jobs.

Although few graduates in either age group had the flexibility to set

Table B-18

Reasons Working in a Job Only Somewhat or Not Related to Undergraduate Major, for Full-Time Employees, by Age

(in percentages)

	Under Age 22	Age 22 or Over
Never planned to take a closely related job	14	8
Prefer work not closely related	10	4
Tried closely related employment, but did not like it	8	6
First job was unrelated to major and became interested in this work	24	19
Joined family business or firm	6	2
Found a better paying job	16	21
Found a job that offers a better chance of career advancement	22	15
Promoted out of closely related job	2	2
Wanted part-time work, flexible hours	2	2
Wanted to work at home	2	4
On temporary assignment (political appointment, Vista, Peace Corps, USIA, and so on)	1	0
Related jobs not available where I live and do not want to move	15	9
In the military	4	2
Could not get a closely related job, but would prefer one	32	19
Limited in job selection by situation of spouse, family responsibilities	10	21
Employment opportunities are scarce for people in related jobs	42	26
N	3,179	53

their own hours, a significant percentage designed their own work programs. More younger than older respondents indicated both that they set their own hours and designed their own work programs. The older respondents were almost twice as likely as the younger to supervise people trained in their fields.

Only about a third of the respondents felt well paid compared with people in other work settings. Older respondents were more likely than their younger counterparts to feel well paid as compared with others at the same job level and place of employment.

Thirty-seven percent of the older workers felt their skills were being fully utilized on the job as compared with 31 percent of their younger counterparts. Experience in the labor force probably accounts for this dif-

Table B-19
Extent of Contribution of Various Experiences to Current or Most Recent Job, for Full-Time Employees, by Age
(in percentages)

	Under Age 22	Age 22 or Over
Particular course(s) in major field	40	39
Other particular courses	21	21
College study in general	35	25
Work experience while in college	24	20
Extracurricular activities while in college	9	8
Formal training program at place of employment	29	23
Formal training or course other than your college program or programs offered by employer	16	25
General on-the-job experience	68	61
Leisure activities	9	5
N	3,861	70

ference. Utilization of skills has been identified as a very important component of overall job satisfaction, but attention must be paid to other job characteristics as well.

Nearly half of the respondents appeared to be satisfied with their current jobs, indicating that they would like to stay with their current employers. Slightly more of the older respondents felt this way.

More of the younger respondents would have liked more training outside of college before they started working.

Current Annual Income

The median income of older respondents was slightly higher ($12,380) than that of younger respondents ($10,500) (see table B-21). It is surprising that the difference was not greater, given that the former had been in the labor force longer and had more experience.

Attitudes toward Work

Another measure of job satisfaction is an individual's attitude toward his or her job. Respondents in both age groups were asked to indicate their feelings regarding a series of attitudinal statements.

Table B-20
Job Characteristics of Full-Time Employees, by Age
(in percentages)

	Under Age 22	Age 22 or Over
Well paid for work compared with persons at the same job level in same place of employment	35	40
Well paid for work compared with persons at the same job level in other work settings	35	31
Well paid for work compared with people in general with the same amount of education	34	37
Supervise people trained in my field	14	23
Most colleagues trained in my field	40	33
Most of the time, set own hours	16	12
Most of the time, design own work program	41	36
Have policy- and decision-making responsibility	45	35
Have sufficient status or prestige in job	47	50
Satisfied with career progress to date	56	60
Current job offers good future prospects for further advancement	46	50
Job fits long-range goals	39	39
Skills are fully utilized in job	31	37
Working at a professional level	60	55
Satisfied with the quality of interaction with supervisor	53	50
Would like to remain with current employer for the forseeable future	46	54
During college had a part-time or summer job related to current job	32	24
Self-employed	4	3
Would have liked more college training before started working	14	14
Would have liked more training outside of college before started working	13	3
Received job training inappropriate for actual job requirements	10	8
Glad had college education	77	78
N	6,242	105

Among those who were employed full time in 1977, the two groups differed little in their attitudes toward work (see table B-22). The statements
with which respondents were most likely to indicate strong agreement were:
"I have the skills necessary to perform my work activities optimally," "If I
had not attended college, I would have been able to perform my current (or

Table B-21
Current Annual Income of Full-Time Employees before Taxes, by Age
(in percentages)

	Under Age 22	Age 22 or Over
None	0	0
Below $7,000	12	9
$7,000-$9,999	32	25
$10,000-$11,999	23	19
$12,000-$13,999	14	18
$14,000-$16,999	12	18
$17,000-$19,999	5	7
$20,000-$24,999	1	1
$25,000-$29,999	0	2
$30,000-$34,999	0	2
$35,000-$39,999	0	0
$40,000 and over	0	0
N	6,268	105
Median income	$10,500	$12,380

most recent) job as well," and "If I get the promotions I expect and can expand my responsibilities as I become more experienced, I would be satisfied to remain in my type of work for the foreseeable future." These attitudes are slightly more characteristic of the younger respondents than of the older ones, probably because new entrants to the labor force often exude self-confidence and are more oriented toward the future. The older respondents were more likely to feel that their jobs did not leave them enough time for outside leisure activities and for their families and friends and that they would reenter college or seek occupational retraining some time after they were 30 years old.

Job Satisfaction

Although at least 50 percent of the respondents in both groups said they were not underemployed (see table B-23) and almost as many said they were very satisfied with their current jobs (see table B-24), only about 40 percent said they were in their preferred occupations (see table B-25).

Older respondents were more satisfied with their jobs than their younger counterparts, and the mean length of employment at their current jobs was three years, five months; younger respondents had been with their jobs for an average of two years, one month. This difference may simply indicate that older respondents had already clarified their career aspirations at

Table B-22
Attitudes of Full-Time Employees toward Work, by Age
(in percentages)

	Under Age 22	Age 22 or Over
My job does not leave me enough time for my family, friends	19	22
My job does not leave me enough time for outside, leisure activities	26	28
If I could find a job with less time demand, I would take it if I didn't have to suffer too great a salary cut	22	19
People with less education are performing the same job I currently (or most recently) performed	41	41
If hired, people with less education would be able to perform the same job I currently (or most recently) performed	40	40
I have the skills necessary to perform my work activities optimally	63	58
If I had not attended college, I would *not* have been able to perform my current (or most recent) job as well	60	55
If I had not attended college, I would have been able to perform my current (or most recent) job as well	30	30
If I had not attended college, I would have been able to perform my current (or most recent) job better	3	0
Prospects are good that I will reenter college or seek occupational training sometime after I am 30 years old	31	38
If I get the promotions I expect and can expand my responsibilities, I would be satisfied to remain in my type of work for the forseeable future	54	48
N	6,325	104

the time they entered college. Most either perfected or modified what they already had.

Substantial proportions of both groups were very satisfied with working conditions (hours and location) and job security (see table B-26). On other points the groups differed. Thus, more older than younger respondents were very satisfied with the challenges their jobs offered, the opportunities for creativity that were available to them, and their opportunities to use their training or schooling in their jobs and to contribute to society through

Table B-23
Perceptions of Underemployment, for Full-Time Employees, by Age
(in percentages)

	Under Age 22	Age 22 or Over
Not underemployed	54	56
Underemployed, but for personal reasons prefer to remain in this or a similar position	13	14
Underemployed, would prefer more challenging position	33	30
N	6,210	102

their jobs. Most of these advantages develop after one has held a job for several years.

Those who were of traditional college age when freshmen were more likely to be very satisfied with their visibility for jobs at other institutions or organizations. Both groups of respondents were about equally satisfied with the other job aspects listed.

Career Plans

Only 14 percent of the younger respondents and 11 percent of the older ones said they had no career plans when they left college (see table B-27). Most of the older respondents said their career plans were exactly the same now as when they left college; most of the younger respondents had changed their career choice at least once while in college.

"For many students, regardless of their ages—choosing a career is not a one-shot operation, rather it is a continuing process of adjustment that ex-

Table B-24
Satisfaction of Full-Time Employees with Current or Most Recent Job, by Age
(in percentages)

	Under Age 22	Age 22 or Over
Not satisfied	15	15
Somewhat satisfied	43	36
Very satisfied	42	49
N	6,286	105

Table B-25
Whether or Not Working in a Preferred Occupation, for Full-Time Employees, by Age
(in percentages)

	Under Age 22	Age 22 or Over
No	59	56
Yes	41	44
N	6,216	103

tends well beyond the educational years'' (Ochsner 1979, p. 15). Neither should the career-counseling role in college then be a ''one-shot operation''; rather, encouragement of alternative career consideration is constantly needed. About a third of the sample said their career plans were somewhat the same now as when they graduated, and a quarter said their plans were not at all the same.

Although most of the respondents did not change their career plans, more of the younger than the older ones had changed their plans (see table B-28). The younger respondents were more likely to say that they had changed career plans after leaving college because they did not know enough about career alternatives when they left college, because jobs in their original career choice were scarce, because they were no longer interested in the same career, or because they decided to go to graduate school. The older respondents were more likely to say that a change in their financial circumstances or in their family responsibilities made a career change necessary.

Satisfaction with Life

Older respondents and married respondents were satisfied with more aspects of life than their younger and single counterparts (see table B-29), perhaps because they had had more time to fulfill their aspirations. Married respondents were less satisfied with the amount of time they had for leisure activities than with other aspects of their lives.

Summary and Implications

Now that we have examined the results of the follow-up data, the value of national data on college graduates' educational and career outcomes is ap-

Table B-26

Degree of Satisfaction of Full-Time Employees with Various Aspects of Current or Most Recent Job, by Age

(percentages responding "very satisfied")

	Under Age 22	Age 22 or Over
Income	26	25
Fringe benefits	43	42
Working conditions (hours, location)	50	57
Status of position	39	43
Status of employing institution/organization	45	43
Autonomy, independence	42	46
Variety in activities	40	41
Policymaking power	18	21
Congenial work relationships	51	49
Competency of colleagues	39	37
Opportunities for different (better) jobs at this institution/organization	24	27
Visibility for jobs at other institutions/organizations	25	21
Challenge	43	48
Extent of responsibility	43	41
Job security	53	52
Opportunity for leisure time	36	37
Opportunity for creativity	30	35
Opportunity to use training or schooling	38	43
Opportunity to contribute to society	35	47
N	6,272	104

parent. Major findings from the data highlighted from this analysis reveal potential inadequacies in the ways traditional colleges and universities deal with older students. These findings have led to suggestions about improvements these institutions can make to attract the needed adult students and to enable them to achieve their educational and career-related aspirations:

1. The primary reason most freshmen gave for attending college was to get a better job. Institutions hoping to attract adults to their programs should place less emphasis on students' personal, intellectual, and social development and more emphasis on career development.

2. Interest in intellectual development and concerns about the job market were important reasons for choosing a college and deciding to attend college. College counselors may not be able to affect whether adults go

Table B-27
Career Plans of Full-Time Employees, by Age
(in percentages)

	Under Age 22	Age 22 or Over
Had no career plans when left college	14	11
Career plans are exactly the same now as when left college	30	49
Changed career choice at least once while in college	40	19
Career plans are somewhat the same now as when left college	39	31
Career plans are not the same as when left college	27	23
N	6,294	100

to college and which ones they attend, but they can influence students' selections of major fields and curricular paths.

3. Although all the respondents were generally satisfied with the kinds of college counseling they received, few were very satisfied. Younger respondents were dissatisfied with the career counseling available to them. This suggests that the quality of counseling services needs to be improved.

4. Intellectual and job-related benefits were the most widely recognized when respondents were asked about the usefulness of a college education.

5. Few of the respondents said they would attend different institutions if they were deciding to attend college today, and approximately one-third of them said that there was a very good chance that they would change their major fields.

6. College counselors have the most contact with students during their senior years when students become serious about career planning. However, at least three-quarters of the students had already chosen their careers by their senior years. Counselors should be more available throughout all of the students' college years.

7. College placement offices were more helpful to younger than older students in finding jobs. Perhaps the adult students did not take advantage of all their colleges could offer them, or perhaps the placement efforts were not geared toward meeting the needs of both younger and older students. Or perhaps adults already had jobs and did not require placement services.

8. More of the adult than the traditional-age respondents said that they were satisfied with their jobs, and the adults tended to stay at their jobs longer than their younger counterparts.

9. Most of the graduates had career plans when they left college. Although the career plans of most adults stayed the same, the younger

Table B-28
Change in Career Plans of Full-Time Employees, by Age
(in percentages)

	Under Age 22	Age 22 or Over
Did not change career plans	37	58
No longer interested in the same career	20	13
Financial circumstances have changed	18	25
Family responsibilities have changed	15	23
More interested in trying to change society	8	6
Less interested in trying to change society	6	4
Decided to go to graduate school	17	5
Decided not to go to graduate school	8	10
Tried that career, but didn't like it	7	3
Jobs in original career choice were scarce	26	21
Didn't know enough about career alternatives when left college	29	14
N	5,886	95

respondents changed their career plans at least once. Adults were probably already established in careers whereas younger graduates were still "shopping around." Choosing a career however is a continuing process of adjustment and career counselors must constantly encourage students to consider alternative careers.

Table B-29
Satisfaction with Various Aspects of Life, by Age
(percentages responding "very satisfied")

	Under Age 22	Age 22 or Over
Life in general	48	51
Family life	53	53
Quality of leisure activities	33	33
Amount of time for leisure activities	29	28
Town in which you live	35	41
Geographic area in which you live	47	53
Climate where you live	42	49
Social life	28	30
Future prospects	42	39
N	8,777	132

Note

1. The data presented here are part of a larger study funded by the National Institute of Education (Grant No. 76-0080). Supplemental funds were also provided by the Rockefeller Foundation and the College Placement Council Foundation.

References

Advisory Panel on Research Needs in Lifelong Learning. *Lifelong Learning During Adulthood*. New York: College Entrance Examination Board, 1978.

American Council on Education. *National Norms for Entering College Freshmen*. Washington, D.C.: American Council on Education, 1970-1972.

Anderson, R.E., and Darkenwald, G.G. *Participation and Persistence in American Education*. New York: The College Entrance Examination Board, 1979.

Anderson, R.E., and Darkenwald, G.G. " The Adult Part-Time Learner in Colleges and Universities: A Clientele Analysis." *Research in Higher Education* 10 (1979).

Arbeiter, S. "Profile of the Adult Learner." *College Board Review* 102 (Winter 1977):20-27.

Astin, A.W. *Preventing Students from Dropping Out*. San Francisco: Jossey-Bass, 1976.

Astin, A.W. *Four Critical Years*. San Francisco: Jossey-Bass, 1977.

Astin, A.W.; King, M.R.; Light, J.M.; and Richardson, G.T. *The American Freshman: National Norms*. Los Angeles: University of California Press, 1973-78.

Astin, A.W., Panos, R.J., and Creager, J.A. *National Norms for Entering College Freshmen*. Washington, D.C.: American Council on Education, 1966-67.

Astin, H.A., ed. *Some Action of Her Own*. Lexington, Mass.: Lexington Books, D.C. Heath and Company, 1976.

Bishop, J., and Van Dyk, J. "Can Adults Be Hooked on College? Some Determinants of Adult College Attendance." *Journal of Higher Education* 48 (1977):39-62.

Boaz, R.L. *Participation in Adult Education: Final Report, 1975*. Washington, D.C.: National Center for Education Statistics, 1978.

Boyer, E.L. "Breaking Up the Youth Ghetto." In *Lifelong Learners—A New Clientele for Higher Education*, ed. D.Y. Vermilye and W. Ferris. San Francisco: Jossey-Bass, 1975.

Breneman, D.W., and Finn, C.E., Jr. eds., *Public Policy and Private Higher Education*. Washington, D.C.: Brookings Institution, 1978.

Bureau of the Census. "Population Characteristics." *Current Population Reports*, Series P-20, No. 335, 1979.

Burkett, J.E. "Higher Education's Growing Edge." *Educational Record* 58 (Summer 1977):259-69.

Campbell, D.F., and Korim, A.S. *Occupational Programs in Four-Year Colleges: Trends and Issues*. Washington, D.C.: AAHE-ERIC/Higher Education Research Report No. 5, 1979.

Cartter, A.M., and Solmon, L.C. "Implications for Faculty." *Change* 8 (September 1976):37-39.

Charner, I. "Union Subsidies to Workers for Higher Education." In *Subsidies to Higher Education: The Issues*, ed. H. Taubman and E. Whalen. New York: Praeger Publishers, 1980.

Charner, I.; Knox, K.; LeBel, A.E.; Levine, H.A.; Russell, L.J.; and Shore, J.E. *An Untapped Resource: Negotiated Tuition-Aid in the Private Sector*. Washington, D.C.: National Manpower Institute, 1978.

Church, M.E. "The Dwindling Enrollment Pool: Issues and Opportunities." In *Students and Their Institutions*, ed. J.W. Peltason and M.V. Massengale. Washington, D.C.: American Council on Education, 1978.

College Entrance Examination Board. *The College Board News*. New York: The College Board, February 1980.

Creager, J.A.; Astin, A.W.; Boruch, R.F.; and Bayer, A.E. *National Norms for Entering College Freshmen*. Washington, D.C.: American Council on Education, 1968.

Creager, J.A.; Astin, A.W.; Boruch, R.F.; Bayer, A.E.; and Drew, D.E. *National Norms for Entering College Freshmen*. Washington, D.C.: American Council on Education, 1969.

Cross, K.P. *The Missing Link: Connecting Adult Learners to Learning Resources*. New York: The College Entrance Examination Board, 1978.

Cross, P., and Valley, J.R. "Nontraditional Study: An Overview." In *Planning Nontraditional Programs*, ed. K.P. Cross, J.E. Valley and Associates. San Francisco: Jossey-Bass, 1976.

Eide, K. "Recurrent Education General Policy Options and Objectives." In *Recurrent Education*, ed. S.J. Mushkin. Washington, D.C.: National Institute of Education, 1973.

Eldred, M.D., and Marienau, C. *Adult Baccalaureate Programs*. Washington, D.C.: AAHE-ERIC/Higher Education Research Report, No. 9, 1979.

Fuller, B. "Addressing Costs and Questioning Benefits." In *Students and Their Institutions*, ed. J.W. Peltason and M.V. Massengale. Washington, D.C.: American Council on Education, 1978.

Gass, J.R. "Recurrent Education: The Issues." In *Recurrent Education*, ed. S.J. Mushkin. Washington, D.C.: National Institute of Education, 1973.

Gibson, D.L. "The Universities and the Part-Time Students: Problems and Prospects, part 2. Part-Time Students: Who are They and What to Do about Them." *Continuum: The National University Extension Association Quarterly* 42 (September 1977):9-11.

Glover, R. In *Alternative Scenarios of the American Future, 1980-2000* ed. Beatrice Gross. New York: The College Entrance Examination Board, 1979.

Green, K.C. "Measuring the Quality of Effort of Adult Learners." Paper presented at the 1980 National Conference of the National Association of Student Personnel Administrators. Los Angeles: Laboratory for Research on Higher Education, University of California, 1980.

Hamilton, B.E. "Community Colleges: Adult Part-Time Students and the Higher Education Act." *Change* (May-June 1978):58-59.

Harrington, F.H. *The Future of Adult Education*. San Francisco: Jossey-Bass, 1977.

Houle, C.O. *The Inquiring Mind*. Madison, Wisc.: University of Wisconsin Press, 1961.

Indiana Commission for Higher Education. *Adult Learning Participation/ Interest Survey: Summary Report*. Indianapolis: January 1979.

Johnstone, J.W., and Rivera, R.J. *Volunteers for Learning*. Chicago: Aldine Publishing Co., 1965.

Knox, A.B. *Adult Development and Learning*. San Francisco: Jossey-Bass, 1977.

Kuh, G.D., and Ardaiolo, F.P. "Adult Learners and Traditional Age Freshmen: Comparing the 'New' Pool with the 'Old' Pool of Students." *Research in Higher Education Journal*, Association for Institutional Research 10 (1979).

Kyle, R.M.J. *Issues in Post-Secondary Education: The Impact of Nontraditional Students*. Washington, D.C.: National Center for Education Statistics, 1979.

Leslie, L.L. "Tax Allowances for Non-Traditional Students." In *The University of Chicago School Review*, ed. D.M. Windham, N. Kurland, and F.H. Levinsohn. 86 (May 1978).

London, J., Wenkert, R., and Hagstrom, W.O. *Adult Education and Social Class*. Berkeley: University of California Survey Research Center, 1963.

Mayhew, L.B. *Surviving the Eighties*. San Francisco: Jossey-Bass, 1979.

McMahon, E.E. *The Emerging Evening College*. Columbia University, Teachers College, 1960.

Mincer, J. "The Determination of Labor Incomes: A Survey with Special Reference to the Human Capital Approach." *Journal of Economic Literature* 8 (1970):1-26.

National Center for Education Statistics. *Fall Enrollment in Higher Education, 1975*. Washington, D.C.: National Center for Education Statistics, 1976.

National Center for Education Statistics. *Participation in Adult Education: Final Report, 1975*. Washington, D.C.: National Center for Education Statistics, 1978a.

National Center for Education Statistics. *Projections of Education Statistics to 1986-87*. Washington, D.C.: National Center for Education Statistics, 1978b.

Ochsner, N.L. "Implications for Counselors from National Student Data." In *Using Longitudinal Data in Career Counseling*, New Directions for Education, Work and Careers, no. 7, L.C. Solmon and N.L. Ochsner, eds., San Francisco: Jossey-Bass, 1979.

Organization for Economic Cooperation and Development. *Recurrent Education: A Strategy for Lifelong Learning*. Paris, France: Center for Educational Research and Innovation, 1973.

O'Keefe, M. *The Adult, Education, and Public Policy*. Palo Alto, Aspen Institute for Humanistic Studies, 1977.

Pace, C.R. *Measuring Quality of Effort*. Los Angeles: Laboratory for Research on Higher Education, University of California, 1979.

Rossman, J.G. *Issues in Post-Secondary Education: Personal Challenges*. Washington, D.C.: National Center for Education Statistics, 1979.

Schlaver, D.E. *The Uncommon School: The Adult Learner in the University*. Ann Arbor: Center for the Study of Higher Education, 1977.

Sheats, P.H. *The Case Against the Adult Dropout*. Boston, Mass.: Center for the Study of Liberal Education for Adults at Boston University, 1965.

Shulman, C.H. *Enrollment Trends in Higher Education*. Washington, D.C.: American Association for Higher Education, 1976.

Solmon, L.C., Ochsner, N.L., and Hurwicz, M. *Alternative Careers for Humanities Ph.D.'s*. New York: Praeger Publishers, 1979.

Stone, G.C. "Higher Education for the Elderly: Continuing in the Mainstream of American Life." *Research in Higher Education* 10 (1979).

Summerskill, J., and Osander, J. "Educational Passport." In *Lifelong Learners—A New Clientele for Higher Education*, ed. D.Y. Vermilye and W. Ferris. San Francisco: Jossey-Bass, 1975.

Weinstock, R. *The Greying of the Campus*. New York: Educational Facilities Laboratories, 1978.

Westervelt, E.M. *Barriers to Women's Participation in Post-Secondary Education: A Review of Research and Commentary as of 1973-74*. Washington, D.C.: National Center for Education Statistics, 1975.

Wiggens, R. "Statistics of the Month: Age Structure of College Enrollment." *American Education* 7 (August-September 1977):34.

Wirtz, W.W. *Formal Occupational Training of Adult Workers*. Washington, D.C.: Manpower/Automation Research Monograph No. 2, 1964.

Wirtz, W.W. *Tuition-Aid Revisited: Tapping the Untapped Resource*. Washington, D.C.: The National Manpower Institute, 1979.

Zeigler, W.C. *Recurrent Education: A Model for the Future of Adult Education and Learning in the United States*. Syracuse: Education Policy Research Center for the National Foundation for Post-Secondary Education, May 1972.

Index

Academic: area patterns, 1, 53-54; attainments, 115-117; counseling, 119-120; course work, 11, 83; degrees, 62-63; involvement, 95; reputations, 31-32, 35-36, 88, 100-101

Accomplishments, scholarly, 82

Achievements: financial, 14, 77, 80-81; high-school, 54

Administration and administrators: college positions, 73, 92; and curricular changes, 5; and guidance, 1; responsibility of, 80-81

Admissions: low, 27, 69; open, 86; of part-time students, 10; requirement procedures, 31, 85; standards for, 27, 69, 86

Adult students in education, 1-5, 16, 41, 96; ages of, 13-14, 86; aspirations of, 62-63, 94; attendance of, 10, 27, 85; baccalaureate programs for, 48; barriers facing, 88; black, 16, 18, 41, 51, 83; in Catholic colleges, 27; C.I.R.P. population, 10, 16; career choices, 72; college choices, 37; in community colleges, 89; decision-making policies, 69; definition of, 2; degree programs for, 48, 93, 97; enrollment status of, 1, 5-6, 9; financial concerns and resources, 25, 39-41, 88-89; four-year institutions, 31; as freshmen, 7, 10, 13, 16, 70, 94; full-time, 25, 37, 41, 52, 72, 85; goals and objectives of, 73-74; learner's characteristics, 1, 3, 7, 23; married, 23-24, 67; and the military, 14; minority, 20; part-time, 2, 5, 9-10, from poor families, 41, 89; population, 4-5, 16, 24, 86; postsecondary studies, 1, 3, 13, 28-29; Protestant colleges, 27; by sex and year, 19; in two-year colleges, 7, 10, 14, 20, 24, 27, 30, 50; undergraduate studies, 4-5; unmarried, 20, 23-24, 44, 49, 67; white, 16, 24, 51

Advisory Panel on Research Needs in Lifelong Learning During Adulthood, 97

Age, factor of, 4, 45, 93. *See also* Traditional-age students

Agencies: funding, 113; private employment, 127

Aggressiveness, verbal, 95

Agriculture, study of, 45, 66-70, 79-80, 112-113

Aid: to adults, 89; family, 42, 44, 47, 89, 104-111; federal programs, 90; financial, 9-10, 14, 20, 32-33, 35-41, 44, 46, 49-50, 85, 87, 89-90, 95, 100-101, 115; gift (nonreturnable), 48; parental, 42, 46; public, 49; scholarship, 48; tuition, 91

American Association for Community and Junior Colleges, The, 86

Anderson, R.E., 2, 27, 73

Annual income, current, 131, 133

Arbeiter, S., 1, 34

Architecture, study of, 70

Ardailo, F.P. 1-2

Armed forces veterans. *See* Military

Artistic: goals and objectives, 74-78; works, 81

Artists and the arts, fine and performing, 45, 68-72, 79-81, 112-113, 116, 128

Aspirations: adult, 62-63, 94; for degrees, 62-62, 94; of women, 63; of young students, 62

Associate's degree in education, 63-67, 116-117

Astin, Alexander W., 48, 50, 62, 94

Athletics, involvement in, 95

Attainment: academic, 115-117; leadership, 82; parents' educational, 24-26

Attendance: college, 4, 9, 14, 22, 27,

Attendance: *(cont.)*
50, 53, 85, 94, 116; of married
students, 22, 85
Attitudes: changes in, 22, 123-124;
societal, 10, 13, 22; work, 131-133
Automobile repairs, study of, 35
Autonomy: factor of, 137; and job
levels, 129

Bachelor of Divinity degree (B.D.),
64-67
Bachelor's degrees (B.A. and B.S.),
62, 64-67, 116-117, 120, 122
Banks, borrowing from, 89
Barriers: adult, 88; institutional, 85
Basic Educational Opportunity Grant
Program (BEOG), 42, 46, 48-50, 90,
104-111
Benefits: consumption, 89; cost ratio,
92; fringe, 91, 137; G.I. Bill, 39, 41,
44, 46, 49-50, 92, 104-111; job-
related, 89, 120, 138; military 47,
89; motivational, 95; social security,
43; societal, 63
Biological sciences: factor of, 45, 66,
79, 112-113; majors in, 46, 68-70,
80
Birthrates, effects of, 77
Bishop, J., 11, 16, 34, 89-90
Black ethnic group, 7, 20-21, 44, 89,
105; adult, 16, 18, 41, 51, 83; colleges for, 11, 14, 17, 19, 23-24,
28-29, 35, 45-46, 62-63, 66, 69,
79-80, 82; financing for, 46;
freshman, 16
Boaz, R.L. 13
Bookstores, 13
Borrowing and borrowers, 89
Boyer, E.L., 89, 91
Breneman, D.W., 87
Burkett, J.E., 91
Business: factor of, 45, 57, 79, 82,
97, 112-113; goals, 78, 80; management, 72; majors, 46, 63, 66, 68-70,
80; ownership, 80; programs, 94;
schools, 92
Businessmen, 71-72, 127-128

Campbell, D.F., 37
Campus activities: elderly on, 1; extended, 97; jobs on, 126; living on,
62-63, 87
Capital theory and theorists, human,
11, 25, 62
Career: advancement, 7, 121-122,
128, 130; changes, 125, 139; choos-
ing of, 72, 125-136; counselors,
116-120, 125-126, 136, 138; deci-
sions, 125; development, 113-114;
goals, 14; occupations, 70-72; plans
and programs, 66, 135-136, 138;
training, 35
Cartter, A.M., 1, 4
Catholic colleges: adults in, 27; four-
year, 11, 28-29, 45, 79
Census, Bureau of the, 3, 9
Charver, I., 91
Chatham College, 87
Chicano ethnic group, 16
Children and child care: cost of, 14,
49, 88; services for, 10, 14, 22, 24
Church, M.E., 1
Churches, influence of, 97
Civil Service, applications for, 126-127
Classification of students, 2
Clergymen, profession of, 71-72, 128
College Entrance Examination Board,
The, 86
Colleges and universities: academic
reputation, 31-32, 35-36, 88,
100-101; administration, 73, 92; attendance at, 4, 9, 14, 22, 27, 50, 53,
85, 94, 116; black, 11, 14, 17, 19,
23-24, 28-29, 35, 45-46, 62-63, 66,
69, 79-80, 82; Catholic, 11, 27-29,
45, 79; choice of, 27-37, 85; community, 1, 57, 86, 88; counseling in,
118-120, 125-126, 138; credit
courses, 57; economic value of,
87-88; environment, 78; experiences,
85, 119-121; four-year, 5, 7, 9-11,
17, 19, 23-24, 27-31, 45, 50, 57,
62-63, 66, 69, 86, 95, 115; junior,
57; liberal-arts, 66, 78; market, 3;
placement offices, 126-127, 138;

preparatory programs, 51-53, 58, 85; private, 11, 27-29, 45, 78; Protestant, 11, 28-29, 45, 78-79; public, 11, 27-30, 44-45, 79; recruitment for, 30, 35, 118; returnees to, 39, 60, 94-96; satisfaction with, 119-121; selectivity reasons for, 30-37; social life in, 123; teachers in, 71-72, 128; technical, 28-29, 45; traditional, 1, 3, 30, 97, 137; two-year, 5, 7, 16-17, 20, 23, 46, 57, 62-63, 78, 86, 88, 115.

Commercial: interest rates, 47; loans, 42

Communications, factor of, 87

Community Action Program, 81

Community centers, 2

Community colleges, 1, 57, 86-89

Commuting distances, 59-60

Compensation hypothesis, 25-26

Competency tests, 93

Composition of music, training for, 74, 78

Confidence, self-, 53, 93-94, 116, 122

Consumer-oriented goals, 75

Consumption benefits, 89

Continuing education unit (CEU), 96-97

Contributions to science, 75-76, 81

Cooperative Institutional Research Program (CIRP), 6, 46, 75, 85, 113; adult population, 10, 16; freshman survey, 31, 73, 85; norms, 7, 29, 47, 54; sampling methods, 10, 13-14, 20, 30, 39, 57, 69, 72, 93

Corporate sector, influence of, 91

Correspondence schools, free, 92

Cost(s): child care, 14, 49, 88; educational, 39; ratio benefits, 92; tuition, 11

Counselors and counseling: academic, 119-120; career, 116-120, 125-126, 138; college, 118-120, 125-126, 138; guidance, 36, 100-101; high-school, 118; remedial programs, 35, 85

Course credit work, 3, 11-12, 58, 85-86, 89, 92-93; noncredit, 57, 97;

refresher, 54

Creativity, influence of, 137

Cross, K. Patricia, 3, 11, 88

Current Population Reports, 3

Curriculum: changes, 5, 37; contents, 38, 97; high-school preparation, 52-53; regular, 2, 96-97

Darkenwald, G.G., 2, 27, 73

Data collection and analysis, 9-10, 39, 85

Day-care facilities, use of, 85

Daytime faculty, regular, 4

Decisions and decision making: adult, 69; career, 125; college, 113-115; responsibilities of, 129, 132

Deferment mortgage-payment plans, 90

Degrees and degree programs, variable, 2-3, 13, 25, 34, 48, 62-67, 71-72, 93-94, 97, 116-117, 120, 122

Demography, factor of, 9-26, 41, 85

Dentists and dental profession, 64-67, 71-72, 117

Depreciation, allowances for, 91

Diploma, high-school, 64

Disadvantaged people, 25

Dissatisfaction, job, 11

Divinity students and studies, 64-67

Divorce: factor of, 22, 24; rate of, 77

Doctoral programs, 1, 62, 117

Doctors: dental, medical, and veterinary, 64-67, 71-72, 117, 128

Dormitory life, college, 60-63, 95

Drop-outs, high-school and college, 34, 39, 48

Earnings: family, 49; increase in, 44; limits on, 47; power of, 121-124; of spouse, 91

Economic system and value of education, 87-88, 96

Education and educational attainments, 45, 66, 79-80, 112-113; expenses, 6, 47, 49, 104-106; goals, 6; opportunities, 96; paid-leave programs, 46, 88, 91-92, 97; of parents, 24, 78-49, 111; postcollege, 62;

Education and educational
   attainments: *(cont.)*
   postsecondary, 25, 73; professional,
   97; recurrent, 96; secondary, 71-72;
   special programs, 31-32, 35-36;
   status connection, 2; therapeutic effects of, 34
Eide, K., 91
Eighteen to twenty-one year olds, 1, 4,
   86
Eighteen to twenty-two year olds, 2, 94
Eldred, M.D., 1, 48
Elementary teachers, 71-72, 128
Eligibility, loans, 50
Employees, full-time, 132, 135, 137-138
Employers, subsidies from, 44, 46,
   91-93
Employment: college, 123-126; full-
   time, 44, 123, 134; length of, 133;
   opportunities for, 34, 128, 130;
   private agencies, 127; public/state
   service, 127; regular, 89; skills
   needed for, 22; self-, 132; status,
   48; summer, 89
Engineers and engineering programs,
   45, 66, 68-72, 79-80, 82, 92,
   112-113, 128
English major, study of, 68-70, 79-80,
   112-113
Enrollment: accelerated, 1; in black
   colleges, 14; in colleges, 77-78;
   decline in, 4, 6, 10, 66, 94; degree
   programs, 25; full-time equivalent
   (FTE), 2-4; non-degree programs, 1;
   post-, 62; status, 5-6, 9, 22-23, 36,
   78; two-year, 24, 85
Entering and reentering adult college
   students, 1, 113-115;
Environment: characteristics, 62;
   college, 78; economic, 77; youth-
   oriented, 119
Ethnic racial backgrounds, 7
Evening college movement, 9, 87, 97
Experience: college, 85, 119-121; learning, 94-95; on-the-job, 129, 131;
   social, 125; work, 131
Extended campus, influence of, 97

Extension programs, 3, 35, 96
External degree programs, 97
Extracurricular activities, 95, 131

Faculty, adjunct, 31; contact, 95; daytime, 4; members, 73; part-time, 87;
   regular, 3-4, 31; tenured, 87; time
   involved, 87
Family: aid, 42, 44, 47, 49, 89, 104-
   111; goals, 78; income levels, 49,
   51; life, 62, 139; objectives, 74,
   76-77; raising, 73-75, 77, 80-81;
   responsibilities, 22, 24, 37, 59, 123,
   128, 130, 136, 139
Farming and farmers, 71-72, 128
Fatherhood, educational attainment of,
   25, 49, 51, 111
Federal: aid, 90; policies and programs, 50, 93
Federally Guaranteed Student Loans
   (FGSL), 47
Fees, course, 89
Female: adult, 5, 44, 110; black, 20-21;
   college, 5, 9, 13-14, 25, 44, 85, 87;
   commitments of, 14; degree aspirations, 63; marital state, 10, 34, 85,
   114; role of, 10; societal expectations, 14, 16
Fifty, matriculation age, 13
Financial: achievements, 74, 77, 80-81;
   aid, 9-10, 14, 20, 32-33, 35-39, 41,
   44, 46, 49-50, 85, 87-90, 95,
   100-101, 115
Financing: black, 46; college educa-
   tion, 6, 39-50, 85; concerns, 40-41,
   88; and marital factor, 22, 41;
   resources, 39-41; responsibilities, 49;
   restrictions, 22
Fine-arts studies, 68-70, 112-113
Finn, C.E., Jr., 87
First choice of colleges, 30-31
First-time freshman class, 12
First-year educational expenses, 42-43,
   46-49, 104-106
Foresters, 71-72, 128
Formal training sessions, 129, 131
Foundations, philanthropic, 91

Four Critical Years (Astin), 94
Four-year colleges, 5, 7, 12, 23-24, 50, 57, 62-63, 66, 86, 95, 115; and adults, 31; attendance at, 9, 85; and blacks, 19; full-time, 17; nonselective, 31; part-time, 10, 17; private, 11, 28-29, 45; Protestant, 11, 28-29, 45, 78-79; public, 11, 27-30; traditional, 27, 30; and whites, 19. *See also* Colleges and universities
Fraternities, 60-63, 95
Freshman: adult, 7, 10, 13, 16, 70, 94; black, 16; characteristics, 27, 94-95, 125; college choices, 30-31; financial concerns, 41, 47; first-time, 12; full-time, 6; part-time, 12; surveys, 31, 73, 85, 113; traditional, 9, 89; year's activities, 4-5, 56
Fringe benefits, 91, 137
Fuller, B., 89
Full-time: attenders, 14, 50, 85; black students, 17; employees, 132-135; 137-138; employment, 44, 123, 134; four-year colleges, 17; freshman, 6; students, 2, 25, 37, 41, 48, 52, 63, 72; two-year colleges, 17; undergraduates, 1
Full-time equivalent (FTE) enrollment, 2-4
Funding: agencies, 113; sources of, 88

Gass, J.R., 96
GED, high-school equivalency, 56-57
Geography, influence of, 27, 139
G.I. (Government Issue) Bill, educational effects of, 4, 39, 41, 43-44, 46-57, 49-50, 90, 92, 104-111
Gibson, D.L., 34
Gifts, factor of, 42, 44, 48, 104-111
Goals: of adults, 73-74; business, 78, 80; career, 14; consumer-oriented, 75; educational, 6, 9; family, 78; immediate, 86; life, 73-83, 85, 94, 122; long-range, 86; personal, 78; social, 78, 80, 83; status, 78, 82; of traditional-age students, 73; vocational, 75

Grade-inflation phenomenon, 54, 86
Grades: high-school, 54-58, 86
Graduate: degrees, 63; schools, 125, 139; studies, 72
Graduates: high-school, 4, 87, 93, 95
Grants, programs for, 42, 44, 46, 48-50, 90, 104-111
Green, K.C., 95
Guidance: administrators, 1; counselors, 36, 100-101

Hagstrom, W.O., 11, 34, 91
Hamilton, B.E., 13
Harrington, F.H., 1-2, 10, 34, 96-97
Harvard University, 35
Health: factor of, 79-80, 82; professions, 66, 68-72, 112-113, 128; sciences, 70
Helping other people, reason for college, 73, 75-76, 80
High school: achievement, 54; counselors, 118; curriculum preparation in, 52-53; diploma from, 63; educational programs offered in, 2, 9, 34, 46, 51-54, 58, 85; equivalency preparation, 56-57
Higher-education institutions, 9, 48, 78
Higher Education Research Institute (HERI), 6, 94, 96, 113
History, subject of, 68-70, 79-80
Hobbies, need for, 83
Home: living at, 32-33, 35-36, 59, 93; living away from, 30, 35-36, 100-101
Homeowners, unemployed, 91
Honors programs, 95
Houle, Cyril, 82
Household: head of, 3; responsiblities, 44
Housing: campus, 62-63; off-campus, 94; student, 60, 63; subsidized, 60, 94
Human-capital theory and theorists, 11, 25, 62
Humanity studies and departments, 66, 68-70, 79-80, 86, 94, 112-113
Hurwicz, M., 87, 94

Idealism, political, 75
Immobility, problem of, 31
Income: annual, 131, 133; and education, 25; family, 49, 51; groups, 48; high, 25; independent of, 44; levels, 7, 46, 137; limitations, 90; low, 44; parental, 41, 45, 58, 51; personal, 41, 44-45; pressures, 25; of spouse, 48
Independence, forms of, 44, 137
Indiana Commission on Higher Education, 2, 34, 51
Inflation, effects of, 50
In-house training programs, 35
Inquiring Mind, The (Houle), 82
Institutions: barriers, 85; characteristics, 94-95; higher education, 9, 48, 78; local, 31; postsecondary, 2-3, 12; reputation and status of, 69-70, 86; traditional, 2-3; urban, 39. See also Colleges and universities
Intellectual development, reason for college, 113, 119, 137-138
Interest rates, factor of, 47
Interviews and interviewers, 93

Job(s): advancement in, 92, 125; and autonomy, 129; benefits, 89, 120, 138; characteristics, 129-132; dissatisfaction, 11; educational leave from, 97; market, 114; and married women, 34; obsolescence depreciation allowance for, 91; off-campus, 91, 126; on-campus, 91, 126; opportunities, 121-122; professional white collar, 11; related activities to, 22, 31-32, 113, 128; responsibilities, 59; satisfaction, 129, 131, 133-135; search methods, 126-127; security, 134, 137; summer, 47-48, 132; training, 37
Johnstone, J.W.C., 3, 11
Junior colleges, 12, 57

Knox, A.B., 1, 11, 13
Korim, A.S., 37

Kuh, G.D., 1-2
Kyle, R.M.J., 35

Labor: force, 25, 116, 130-131; market, 75; unions, 91
Laboratory work assignments, 95
Lawyers and legal programs, 64-67, 71-72, 128
Leadership abilities, 82, 122
Learning and learners: adult characteristics, 1, 3, 7; experiences, 94-95; lifelong, 94-97; orientations, 82
Leave policies for study programs, 46, 88, 91-92, 97
Leisure-time activities, 25, 37, 50, 83, 89, 94, 133-134, 136-137, 139; of affluent adults, 26
Leslie, L.L., 39
Liberal-arts colleges, 66, 78
Liberal-arts departments, 66, 97
Libraries, use of, 13, 95. See also Bookstores
Life: family, 62, 139; goals, 73-83, 85, 94, 122; learning processes in, 94-97; philosophy of, 73, 75, 77; priorities in, 6; satisfaction with, 136, 139
Living: costs, 90; at home, 32-33, 35-36, 59, 93; away from home, 30, 35-36, 100-101; off campus, 95; on campus, 62-63; with spouses, 60; standards, 90
Loans: commercial, 42; eligibility for, 50; FGSL, 47; NDEA, 44; programs for, 42, 46, 48, 95, 104-111; student, 47, 104-111; subsidized, 47, 90
London, J., 11, 34, 91
Loneliness, factor of, 82

Major subjects in education, 68-70; in four-year colleges, 69; nontechnical, 82; preprofessional, 80; in two-year colleges, 69; undergraduate selection, 118-119
Management: business, 72; programs in, 87
Marienau, C., 1, 48

Marital status, factor of, 20-24, 45, 49, 59, 63, 69, 79, 100-102, 108-112, 120

Market: college, 3; labor, 75

Marriage, state of, 3, 24, 44, 60; financial restrictions of, 22; and women, 10, 34, 85, 114

Master's degree programs and awards, 62-67, 116-117

Mathematics, study of, 66, 68-70, 79, 112-113

Mayhew, L.B., 87

McMahon, E.E., 87, 95, 97

Medical programs and practitioners, 64-67, 117. *See also* Doctors

Metropolitan areas, 16

Mexican-Americans, influence of, 16

Military: benefits, 47, 89; service, 4, 13-14, 43-44, 46, 49, 97, 104-111. *See also* G.I. (Government Issue) Bill

Mincer, J., 11

Minority: backgrounds, 9; group members, 20, 46, 51, 86; postsecondary education, 16; and racial overtones, 7

Mobility: constrained, 44; factor of, 34; socioeconomic, 89

Money, accumulation of, 113-114

Morale, factor of, 91

Mortgage payment deferment program, 90

Motherhood, educational background of members, 25, 45, 78-79

Motivation of college students, 62, 81-82, 95

Music, study and composition of, 74, 78

National Defense Education Act, 42, 44, 47

National Direct Student Loans, 47

National productivity, 89

Noncampus facilities, 60

Noncredit courses, 57, 97

Nondegree programs, enrollment in, 1-2

Nonreturnable (gift) aid, 48

Nonselective four-year colleges, 31

Nontechnical subject matter, 68-70, 79, 82

Nontraditional: coursework, 85; students, 2, 13

Nurses, profession of, 70-72, 128

Objectives: artistic, 74-76, 78; business, 74, 76-77; family, 74, 76-77; personal, 74, 76-78; social, 74, 76; status, 76; of traditional-age students, 75

Obsolescence, job, 91

Occupation(s): career, 70-72; current, 127; programs, 37; retraining for, 133; traditional-age students', 70

Ochsner, N.L., 87, 94, 114, 118, 136

Off-campus: jobs, 91, 126; housing, 94; living, 95; teaching, 87

O'Keefe, M., 34-35, 89, 91

On-campus: jobs, 91, 126; living, 62-63

On-the-job: experience, 129, 131; training, 11, 92

Open-admissions policy, 86

Opportunities: educational, 96; employment, 34, 128, 130; equal, 16; job, 121-122, labor market, 75; work, 87

Osander, J., 97

Organization for Economic Cooperation and Development, The, 96

Overachievers, problems of, 116

Ownership, business, 80

Pace, C. Robert, 95

Parental: aid, 42, 46; educational attainment, 24-26, 49, 51, 111; families, 49; income, 41, 45, 48, 51; living quarters, 60, 62; military service, 44

Part-time: admissions, 10; black colleges, 17; Community colleges, 57; enrollments, 23, 52; faculties, 87; four-year colleges, 10, 17; junior colleges, 57; students, 2, 7, 9-10,

24-25, 41, 48, 97; two-year colleges, 17; work and workers, 31, 47, 50, 123
Peace Corps, 74-76, 130
Performing arts, 81
Perseverance and persistence rates, 62, 73, 122
Personal: characteristics, 78, 93; counseling, 119-120; goals, 78; income, 41, 44-45; interviews, 93; objectives, 74, 76-78; savings, 43, 47, 89, 104-111
Philanthropy, factor of, 91
Philosophy, degrees in, 64-67
Philosophy of life, development of, 73-77
Physical sciences and physics courses, 66, 68-70, 86, 112-113
Placement offices, college employment, 126-127, 138
Plans: career, 66, 135-136, 138; college, 59-72, 85
Policymakers, 93, 132, 137
Political: affairs, 73-75, 81; science, 68-70, 112-113; structure, 76, 81
Population: reports, 5; student, 4, 16, 24, 51, 86
Postcollege education, 62
Postgraduate degrees, 49, 59
Postsecondary education: adult access to, 1, 3, 13, 28-29; changes in, 6-7; experiences in, 73; institutions, 2-3, 11-12; minority-group members, 16; part-time schools, 57; traditional students in, 28-29; unmarried men in, 22; women in, 14, 25
Poverty, effects of, 41, 46, 89
Preparatory Programs, college, 51-54, 58, 85
Preprofessional majors, 45-46, 68-70, 79-80, 112-113
Private: employment agency, 127; four-year colleges, 11, 28-29, 45; liberal-arts colleges, 78; two-year colleges, 11, 28-29; universities, 27-29, 44-45
Professional: contacts, 126; degrees,

62-63, 125; educational, 66, 68-72, 97, 112-113, 128; levels of, 88, 129, 132; schools, 114, 118-119; white-collar jobs, 11, 34
Promotions, business, 11, 133-134
Protestant colleges, 11, 27-29, 45, 78-80
Psychology, study of, 34, 71-72
Public: aid, 49; colleges, 11, 27-30, 44-45, 79; employment services, 127; subsidies, 48-49
Puerto Rican-American racial groups, 16

Quality of institutions, 69-70
Questionnaires, use of, 9, 13, 22, 63, 75, 128

Racial: backgrounds, 16-20, 24; understanding, 81-82
Raising a family, educational incentive, 73-75, 77, 80-81
Reading programs, informal, 96
Reality testing, mechanism for, 93
Reasons for selecting type of college, 30-37
Recreation and facilities for, 62
Recruitment policies and teams, 30, 35-36, 118, 127
Recurrent education, 96
Refresher college courses, 54
Regular: employment positions, 89; faculty members, 3-4, 31
Regulations and restrictions: financial, on married couples, 22; unemployment, 90; university, 85
Religion and control of colleges, 30
Remedial educational help, 9, 35, 51, 53-54
Remission programs: employer subsidies, 91; tuition, 46, 91-92
Reputation: academic, 31-32, 35-36, 88, 100-101; institutional, 69
Research: scientific, 71-72, 127-128; undergraduate participation, 95
Residency requirements, degree, 85, 97
Resident halls, college campus, 62, 95

Resources, financial accessibility to, 39-41

Responsibility: administrative, 80-81; decision-making, 129, 132; family related, 22, 24, 37, 59, 123, 128, 130, 136, 139; financial, 49; household, 44; job-related, 59; traditional, 85

Retraining, occupational, 133

Returning students: adults, 1, 39, 60, 94-96, 113-115; women, 85

Rivera, R.J., 3, 11

Rossmann, J.G., 2

Salaries, increases in, 11

Satisfaction, 73; with college experiences, 119-121; of full-time employees, 132, 135, 137-138; job, 129, 131, 133-135; with life, 136, 139

Savings: accumulation of, 89; increased earnings on, 44; inflation effects on, 50; personal, 43, 47, 89, 104-111; and work, 46, 49, 104-111

Schlaver, D.E., 2, 11, 27, 41, 97

Scholarships, 42, 44, 82, 104-111; state, 48

Schools: business, 92; graduate, 125, 139; postsecondary part-time, 57; professional, 114, 118-119

Science(s): biological, 45-46, 66, 68-70, 79-80, 112-113; contribution to, 75-76, 81; health, 70; laboratory work, 95; political, 68-70, 112-113; social, 34, 66, 68-70, 79-80, 82, 112-113

Scientists, research, 71-72, 127-128

Search methods, 126-127

Secondary educators, 71-72

Security: job, 134, 137; social, benefits, 43

Self-confidence: differences in, 32, 122; lack of, 93-94, 116

Self-discipline, 122

Self-employment, 132

Senior educational years, 125-126

Separation, marital and problems of, 22, 24

Service(s): child-care, 10, 14, 22; employment, 127; military, 4, 13-14, 43-44, 46, 49, 97, 104-111

Sex, preferential differences by, 10, 13-16, 45, 63, 78, 82-83

Sheats, P.H., 91

Shulman, C.H., 2, 39

Sixty and beyond, age of, 13

Skills: acquiring of, 34; adult respondents, 19; employment needs, 22; utilization of, 129, 131

Social: development, 113, 137; experience, 125; fraternities, 95; goals, 78, 80, 83; life, 50, 123, 139; objectives, 74, 76; sciences, 45, 66, 68-70, 79-80, 82, 112-113; security benefits, 43; values, 76, 81

Society: American, 77; attitudes in, 10, 13, 22; benefits for, 63; changes in, 139; contributions to, 134, 137; expectations of women in, 14, 16; technological, 35

Socioeconomic: background characteristics, 45, 78; mobility, 89; traits, 41

Socioeconomic status (SES), low, 25-26, 49, 51, 78

Solmon, Lewis, C., 4, 87, 94

Sororities and sorority houses, 60-63, 95

Sources, financial, 46

Special educational programs, 31-32, 35-36

Spouse: income of, 48, 91; living with, 60

Standards: acceptable, 93; admissions, 27, 69, 86; living, 90; lowering of, 93

State: employment agencies, 127; scholarships, 48

Statistics, factor of, 66-70, 112-113

Status: educational, 2, 94, 129, 137; employment, 48; enrollment, 5-6, 9, 17, 22, 36, 78; goals, 76-78, 82; institutions, 86; marital, 24

Student: adult, 1, 4, 16, 24-25, 51, 62, 86, 113-115; affairs, 7; aspirations,

Student: *(cont.)*
62; definition of, 2; entering and
reentering, 1, 7, 113-115; faculty interaction, 95; four-year colleges, 27,
30; governmental bodies, 95; housing facilities, 60, 63; high-school, 2;
income, 25; involvement by, 94-95;
loans of, 42, 47, 104-111; motivations of, 62, 81-82, 95; objectives,
75; occupations, 70; part-time, 2, 7,
9-10, 20, 25, 41, 48, 97; population,
4, 16, 24, 51, 86; racial
backgrounds, 20; traditional-age,
1-10, 16, 20, 22, 27, 30, 39, 41, 46,
48, 50-51, 54, 70, 75, 85, 88, 93, 96,
116, 123; two-year college, 30;
undergraduate, 5; unmarried, 22
Study: graduate, 72; individualized, 97
Subsidies: of adults, 89; employer, 44,
46, 91-93; of housing, 60, 94; loans,
47, 90; public, 48, 90; of youth, 41
Summer: jobs, 47-48, 89, 104-111, 132;
schools, 97
Summerskill, J., 97
Supplemental Educational Opportunity
Grants (SEOG), 48, 104
Surveys, results of, 31, 73, 85, 93,
113
Swimming instruction, 2

Tables, graphs and charts,6, 10-12,
14-19, 21-23, 28-30, 32-33, 36, 40,
42-45, 52-55, 57-58, 60-61, 63-64,
66-72, 74, 79-81, 100-112, 115,
117-118, 120-139
Tax credits, 91
Teaching and teachers: college, 71-72,
128; elementary, 71-72, 128; off-
campus, styles, 97; tenure, 87
Technical: institutions, 28-29, 45, 57;
major subjects, 46, 68-70, 79, 82
Technology, factor of, 35
Tenure of teaching faculty, 87
Tests and testing: competency, 93;
high-school scores, 86; mechanism
for reality in, 93
Therapeutic effects of education, 34

Thirty-five and over age group, 4-5
Traditional: colleges, 1-3, 97, 137;
curricula, 96; degrees, 3; financial
concerns, 40-41, 88; freshman, 9,
89; students, 13, 16, 28-29
Traditional-age students, 1-10, 16, 22,
27, 39, 51, 44, 46, 48, 50-51, 54, 85,
88, 93, 96, 113, 116, 119, 123, 125,
135; definition of, 2; in four-year
colleges, 30; goals of, 73, 75; occupation of, 70; racial backgrounds,
20; white, 18; women, 87
Training, 134, 137; career-related, 35;
formal, 129, 131; job-related, 37;
on-the-job, 11, 35, 92
Traits, socioeconomic, 41
Transfer of credits, problems of, 86
Transitional programs, 85
Travel, incentives to, 121-122
Tuition, 89; aid for, 91; college, 16,
115; costs, 11; low, 32-33, 35-37,
39, 100-101; remission programs,
46, 91-92; and tax-credit, 91
Tutoring, need for, 54
Twenty-five years and older, 16
Twenty-five to thirty-four age group,
4-5
Twenty-four and under, 5
Twenty-one years and older, 13
Twenty-six years and older, 13-14
Twenty-two to thirty-four years age
group, 4
Twenty-two to twenty-five years age
group, 13, 14, 24
Two-year colleges, 5, 16-17, 23, 46, 57,
62-63, 78, 88, 115; adults in, 7, 10,
14, 20, 24, 27, 30, 50; attendance
at, 9; black students, 19; enrollment
in, 24, 85-86; major subjects in, 69;
part-time students, 17; private, 11,
28-29; public, 11, 28-29, 44-45, 79;
traditional age students in, 30

Underachievers, educational, 116
Underemployment, perceptions of,
133, 135
Undergraduate: education, 4-5; major

subjects, 118-119; research participation, 95; students, 5

Unemployment and the unemployed: return to school, 34-35; regulations, 90-91

Unions, 93; courses sponsored by, 92; labor, 91

Universities. *See* Colleges and universities, 27-29, 44-45

Unmarried adult students, 20, 22-24, 44, 49, 67

Urban institutions, 39

Valley, J.R., 3, 11
Values, social, 76, 81
Van Dyk, J., 11, 16, 34, 89-90
Verbal aggressiveness, 95
Veterinarian studies, 64-67, 117
Vietnam War, 39; veterans of, 4, 92
Vista program, 74-76, 130
Vocational: activities, 22, 86-87, 97, 116; goals, 75; schools, 57

Wealth and the rich, 26, 46
Weinstock, R., 1
Wenkert, R., 11, 34, 91
Westervelt, E.M., 14, 48, 59
White-collar jobs, professional, 11, 34

White ethnic group: college population, 7, 16, 21, 24, 51, 104; four-year colleges, 19; traditional, 18; two-year colleges, 19

Widows, factor of, 22, 24

Wiggins, R., 13

Wirtz, W.W., 11, 91

Women, 10, 114; expectations of, 14, 16; job-related activities, 34; return to education, 14, 25, 85; traditional college age, 87

Word-of-mouth information, 30, 35-36

Work: attitude toward, 131-133; college, 42; experience, 131; and major subject, 128; market, 114; opportunities, 89; part-time, 31, 47, 50, 123; and savings, 46, 49, 104-111; and study, 48; summer, 47-48, 89, 104-111, 132

Writing ability, 122

Young Men's Christian Association (YMCA), 97

Youth-oriented environment, 62, 119; subsidization of, 41

Ziegler, W.C., 96

About the Authors

Lewis C. Solmon received the B.Com. in 1964 from the University of Toronto and the Ph.D. in economics in 1968 from the University of Chicago. He is currently a professor in the Graduate School of Education at the University of California at Los Angeles, secretary/treasurer of the Higher Education Research Institute in Los Angeles, and president of the Human Resources Policy Corporation. In October 1978 he was selected by *Change* as one of the 100 young leaders of American higher education.

His books include *Economics; Does College Matter?; Male and Female Graduate Students: The Question of Equal Opportunity; Capital Formation by Expenditures on Formal Education, 1880 and 1890; College as a Training Ground for Jobs*; and *Alternative Careers for Humanities PhDs*. He has published numerous articles in economics and education and has served on a number of national advisory panels dealing with education and career development.

Joanne J. Gordon received the B.A. in sociology in 1978 from the University of California at Los Angeles. She is currently a research analyst at the Higher Education Research Institute in Los Angeles. Ms. Gordon has been involved in several studies covering such topics as the nature of master's degrees in the humanities, the sciences, and engineering fields and the relationship of college education to career development.